THE**CITY**

D1719460

Praise for *The City*

"David Busic's *The City* is a provocative dare not just to the Church of the Nazarene but also to the larger Wesleyan-Holiness family in the United States and Canada. This book challenges us to revisit our past and our frame for the future; it begs us to re-pivot and seize twenty-first-century opportunity, as did the first-century Acts of the Apostles. Busic's argument for urban focus is persuasively grounded in fresh exegesis of Scripture, history, society, and culture. More than just another call to action, it is a challenge to reunite our passion for souls and a vision to transform the world around us. Read it. Ask the Holy Spirit to help you think about it. Read it again. Then, do something about it. A desperate world is waiting."

Jim Lyon
General Director
Church of God Ministries

"With precision born out of a love for the message of holiness and a love for the city, David Busic has written a timely treatise that provides not only the rationale for ministry to the urban core but also a map to guide our mission back to this neglected frontier. *The City* reminds us of the passion Jesus had for people and cities, and rekindles the vision of John Wesley and Phineas Bresee for this important work."

David W. Bowser
Mid-Atlantic District Superintendent
Church of the Nazarene

"At a time when American cities are thriving and full of opportunity for ministry, the church is too often on the sidelines. David Busic has artfully interwoven church history, theology, Scripture, sociology, and missiology in ways that are informative, innovative, and instructive for the mission of the church in the city. *The City* is an important and timely book, especially for Wesleyan pastors and lay leaders. It is well-written and accessible. Timely and important. Join the conversation in thinking creatively about ministry in the American urban context."

Ron Benefiel
Dean, School of Theology and Christian Ministry
Point Loma Nazarene University

"*The City* accomplishes the nearly impossible—to be both prophetic and hopeful. It arises out of the optimistic grace deeply rooted in Wesleyan-Holiness DNA. It is evident that Busic deeply loves the church, so he calls her to what is best and perhaps hardest. The internationalization of cities and the strength of the millennial generation adds momentum to the deep biblical and theological conviction that God is providing a fresh opportunity to be a transforming presence in the city. While David suggests some practical approaches to stimulate thinking, there is a movement-over-model spirit in his writing that frees readers to be endlessly creative as the Spirit empowers us."

Wayne Schmidt
General Superintendent
The Wesleyan Church

"David Busic takes us through the history of the Wesleyan-Holiness movement. From the earliest days, he chronicles our path to the city, and tragically, our retreat from it. Busic lays the theological groundwork for the church to return to and thrive in the city. God truly is the God of the city. *The City* is a must-read, for we are all called to care for the city, and the hope for the city is our theology!"

Jay Height
Executive Director, Shepherd Community Center
Indianapolis, Indiana

"In this turbulent period of cultural, structural, and economic change accentuated by the rapid urbanization of our world, the Christian faith has rarely had a more urgent spiritual and moral responsibility to live and proclaim its truths. Similarly and in particular, Busic argues, the Wesleyan-Holiness heritage has never had a greater opportunity to affirm and clearly present to the reemerging urban world—especially to those on the margins—a hope-laden message of personal and social transformation. This is not a new agenda, yet neither is it easily embraced, as attested by Busic in this book. Indeed, *The City* should be read as a clarion call to those within the Wesleyan-Holiness movement to fully embody its missional ecclesiology—not to recapture what was but to discern creative ways to carry out contextual, faithful, and bold ministries in the ever-evolving urban landscape."

Michael Mata
Urban Missiologist
Pastor for Community Engagement
Los Angeles First Church of the Nazarene

THE**CITY**

Urban Churches in the
Wesleyan-Holiness Tradition

DAVID A. BUSIC

THE FOUNDRY
PUBLISHING

Copyright © 2020 by David A. Busic
The Foundry Publishing
PO Box 419527
Kansas City, MO 64141
thefoundrypublishing.com

978-0-8341-3928-2

Printed in the
United States of America

All rights reserved. No part of this publication may be reproduced, stored in a retrieval system, or transmitted in any form or by any means—for example, electronic, photocopy, recording—without the prior written permission of the publisher. The only exception is brief quotations in printed reviews.

Cover Design:Rob Monacelli
Interior Design: Kevin Williamson

Library of Congress Cataloging-in-Publication Data

A complete catalog record for this book is available from the Library of Congress.

All Scripture quotations, unless indicated, are taken from The Holy Bible, *New International Version*® (NIV®). Copyright © 1973, 1978, 1984, 2011 by Biblica, Inc.® Used by permission. All rights reserved worldwide.

Scripture quotations marked (MSG) are taken from *The Message* (MSG). Copyright © 1993, 2002, 2018 by Eugene H. Peterson. Used by permission of NavPress. All rights reserved. Represented by Tyndale House Publishers, Inc.

The internet addresses, email addresses, and phone numbers in this book are accurate at the time of publication. They are provided as a resource. The Foundry Publishing does not endorse them or vouch for their content or permanence.

10 9 8 7 6 5 4 3 2 1

Contents

ACKNOWLEDGMENTS

As with life, there is no such thing as a book without many contributors. My interest in the city began through the influence of a father-figure mentor who served as the district superintendent of churches in and around San Francisco. Clari Kinzler would often say, "David, don't forget about our cities. We have to reach our cities. Our theology works in the city." Now in his eighties, Clari's vision for the church is as fresh as it has ever been.

My friend and longtime accountability partner, Ron Benefiel, instilled in me a passion for the history and work of the Church of the Nazarene in the city. His unwavering belief in the Wesleyan-Holiness message and his deep commitment to the poor inspire me to faithfulness.

Thank you to Julie Burch and Laura Lighthill, whose careful editing always makes my writing sound better than I ever could alone.

Thank you to Bonnie Perry, editorial director *par excellence*, who models the Barnabas life as well as anyone I know and who persistently reminds me, "David, you are the one to write this."

Thank you to Chris Pollock and Michaele LaVigne for making me feel as though my mentorship matters. Additionally, Michaele's end-of-chapter questions and mini features of urban practitioners offer an on-the-ground understanding of the diversity of ways there are for the church to engage the city.

Thank you to my now-adult children, Megan, Ben, and Madison, for giving us the pure joy of being our best of friends, and to Christi, for everything else.

A NOTE
FROM THE AUTHOR

As you will soon discover, footnotes are intentionally plentiful throughout this book. I owe a great debt to the plethora of urban-centric thinkers, writers, and pioneer practitioners who have gone before me. I encourage you to consider the footnotes carefully, both for further study and for insights offered outside the body of the main text. For the sake of convenience, full citations are offered each time a new chapter begins, even if that author or resource has been cited previously.

INTRODUCTION

"It had been my long-cherished desire to have a place in the heart of the city, which could be a center of holy fire, and where the gospel could be preached to the poor."

—*Phineas Bresee*

The Church of the Nazarene originated in 1895 in Los Angeles, California, under the leadership of Phineas F. Bresee, who is widely considered to be the denomination's founder. Bresee left a prominent position in the Methodist Episcopal Church to work with the poor and addicted on Skid Row in the urban core of Los Angeles. One of his journal entries read, "It had been my long-cherished desire to have a place in the heart of the city, which could be made a center of holy fire, and where the gospel could be preached to the poor."[1]

After an all-night session of prayer by the founding leaders, a layperson named J. P. Widney (second president of the University of Southern California) suggested the name "Church of the Nazarene." The name would be a symbolic witness that the fledgling church would be identified with that aspect of Jesus's ministry devoted to those who were underserved and who had been pushed to the margins—and so the church received its name.[2] The minutes of the organizational

---

1 E. A. Girvin, *Phineas F. Bresee: A Prince in Israel, a Biography* (Kansas City, MO: Nazarene Publishing House, 1916), 99. Quoted in Floyd Cunningham, ed., Stan Ingersol, Harold E. Raser, and David P. Whitelaw, *Our Watchword and Song: The Centennial History of the Church of the Nazarene* (Kansas City, MO: Beacon Hill Press of Kansas City, 2009), 96.

2 Harold E. Raser, "Beating Back the Amnesia: Love for Neighbors in the Church of the Nazarene, 1975–1998," presented October 29–30, 1998, Nazarene Compassionate Ministries Conference Theological Symposium, published in *Didache: Faithful Teaching* (February 25, 2008), http://didache.nazarene.org/index.php/regiontheoconf/ncm-1998/739-ncm1998-5-raser/file.

meeting for the First Church of the Nazarene of Los Angeles, California—dated October 30, 1895—state the following:

> Feeling clearly called of God to the carrying on of his work in the conversion of sinners, the sanctification of believers and the building up in holiness of those who may be committed to our care we associate ourselves together as a church of God under the name of the Church of the Nazarene. . . . The field of labor to which we feel especially called is in the *neglected quarters of the cities* and wherever also may be found waste places and souls seeking pardon and cleansing from sin. . . . [This work we aim to do through the agency of] city missions, evangelistic services, house-to-house visitation, caring for the poor, comforting the dying.[3]

With this statement, Bresee—and the other Nazarenes who joined him on this quest—launched an urban movement.

The commitment of the Church of the Nazarene to the cities brought a resurgence of interest in the masses by many other groups and churches and was a viable motivation through the early years of the new denomination. It was both theologically and socially motivated. However, as time went by, the church-growth concept of "redemption and lift"[4] brought about a developing tendency for city churches to relocate to the suburbs, where their members were moving.

Paul Benefiel, a former district superintendent of the Los Angeles District Church of the Nazarene and a sociologist by training, suggested the Church of the Nazarene may have been moving away from Bresee's original purpose as early as 1901.[5] This supposition is supported by a statement Bresee wrote in the *Nazarene Messenger* dated December 31, 1901: "The evidence of the presence of Jesus in our midst is that we bear the gospel, particularly to the poor. This must be genuine; it is more than sentiment; it cannot be simulated nor successfully imitated."[6] Two months earlier, in October 1901, Bresee wrote, "The first miracle

---

3 Local Church Minutes, "Meeting of the Congregation," Los Angeles (October 30, 1895), 3–4. Quoted in Cunningham et al., *Watchword and Song*, 100. Emphasis added.

4 Donald A. McGavran, *Understanding Church Growth* (Grand Rapids: Wm. B. Eerdmans Publishing Co., 1970), 295. McGavran coined the phrase "redemption and lift" to describe the power of the gospel to transform every person—particularly their socioeconomic state.

5 Paul Benefiel, "Nazarenes in the City: The Strategy for Los Angeles." Paper presented to the Association of Nazarene Social Researchers Conference, 1986. ANSR Collection, Nazarene Archives, Lenexa, KS.

6 Quoted in Harold Ivan Smith, *The Quotable Bresee* (Kansas City, MO: Beacon Hill Press of Kansas City, 1983), 167–68.

after the baptism with the Holy Ghost was wrought upon a beggar. It means that the first service of a Holy Ghost-baptized church is to the poor; its ministry is to those who need them the most. As the Spirit was upon Jesus to preach the gospel to the poor, so his Spirit is upon his servants for the same purpose."[7]

Again, Paul Benefiel affirms, "Although the founding fathers of the Church of the Nazarene saw that their primary ministry was to the poor and to the cities, it is also apparent that the churches of this denomination were generally moving away from the poor and out of the cities. Most churches were not able to cope with the turmoil, the tension, and the frustrations of the inner city."[8] Both internal and external forces changed the original trajectory of emphasis on the urban poor and the welfare of cities.

In addition to these early beginnings, another vision was emerging, according to Timothy L. Smith, a historian from Johns Hopkins University who wrote the preeminent history of the Church of the Nazarene. Masterfully weaving the denominational story, Smith maintained that the early years of the Church of the Nazarene were forged out of compromise between two similar—but slightly different—visions of the Christian life. The resulting outcome alternated between a creative tension and a source of conflict. In Smith's words, "Neither the origin nor the subsequent history of the Church of the Nazarene can be understood without a knowledge of the two holiness traditions, *urban* and *rural*."[9]

The distinguishing characteristics that Smith saw in the urban-holiness leavening of the church, primarily from the northern influence, included an inclination to education with an understanding of and empathy for original Wesleyanism as found in the theological teachings and social reforms of John Wesley. The northern centers of ecclesiastical strength were primarily in cities or closely outlying suburbs. By contrast, the southern group was predominantly rural and took a rigorous stand against formality and worldliness. Their propensity was more focused on aggressive evangelism, the personal crisis of entire sanctification in a believer's life, and a strong influence of the camp meeting ethos from the nineteenth-century Holiness Movement.

7 Quoted in Smith, *The Quotable Bresee*, 167–68.
8 Benefiel, "Nazarenes in the City."
9 Timothy L. Smith, *Called unto Holiness, Volume 1: The Story of the Nazarenes: The Formative Years* (Kansas City, MO: Nazarene Publishing House, 1962), 27. Emphasis added.

This tenuous union between the urban and rural Holiness traditions was considered a miracle by many and, as Smith observes, was key to understanding Nazarene DNA. However, it has continued to be a persistent tension through the years within the structure, polity, and strategy of the denomination. While the emphases from northern and southern Nazarenes were not wrong, the polarity shift had a profound impact on the urban movement of the Church of the Nazarene. By the second generation, the Nazarene missional focus had shifted almost exclusively to suburban and rural areas.

The Church of the Nazarene has greatly evolved from those early days, but the divergent paths in the denomination's beginnings remain. Can a new path be forged for an urban-minded church to coexist with a revivalistic, church-growth-minded church? Can a rural-minded church reorient itself to reach the great urban centers of the world? If the Church of the Nazarene was formed by the merging of two distinct Holiness traditions—urban and rural—then the Lord of the church can also help disparate traditions rediscover a healthy tension going forward.[10]

The purpose of this book is to develop new ways of thinking about missional strategies for church planting, development, and renewal in the urban context. Though the predominant worldview focuses on the Church of the Nazarene, this book considers how a robust missional theology, rooted in the best of the Wesleyan-Holiness tradition, can take shape in a rapidly growing urban context of diverse ecclesial traditions and denominational structures. Additionally, a review of Nazarene experiences and behaviors—some exceptional and some deficient—will aid us in examining how theological practices can nourish and promote a vibrant church-planting movement for those who are Wesleyan at heart.[11]

The World Health Organization projects that by 2030, six out of ten people will live in a city, and by 2050, this proportion will increase to seven out of ten people. These projections almost double the global urban population to 6.4 billion people. Leigh Gallagher reports that, according to census data, the largest

---

10 These disparate traditions are more than geographical. They also include the important factors of class, education, culture, and race, and these differences require thorough parsing.

11 The term "Wesleyan-Holiness" is distinguished from Keswick Holiness (also known as the Higher Life Movement), or Oberlin-Holiness, or Pentecostal Holiness. "Wesleyan" is important as a modifier of "Holiness" in order to differentiate which of the four streams of the American Holiness Movement one is referencing.

American cities "grew at a faster rate [from 2010 to 2011] than their suburbs for the first time in one hundred years."[12]

As the Church of the Nazarene has become more affluent and has risen in socioeconomic status in the past few decades, it has become effective in reaching suburban and rural areas. While urban-suburban lines are blurred in some locales, ministry to city cores has not fared well. This is a troubling reality, especially in light of the recent predictions of urban growth that do not bode well for the future mission of the Church of the Nazarene if current trends are not reversed. If Nazarenes still believe they are called to the "neglected quarters of the cities," as declared in those local church minutes from L.A. in 1895, and if the census predictions and projections are correct about the impending resurgence of urban life in the near future, then the Church of the Nazarene can position itself to take advantage of a significant opportunity for mission by reclaiming the founding members' mission of engagement in and with the city.

Cities are centers of cultural diversity. Cities drive regional and global economies. Cities are the educational, artistic, and technological shapers of society. If globalization means "that one nation's cultural values and paradigms now have the capacity to infiltrate and affect the entire global community," then cities are the framework for it.[13] But cities remain a challenge for many churches because they are expensive, complex, and secularized. For these and other reasons, the majority of the world's great cities are vastly under-churched today.

The most significant Nazarene works that remain in the urban context are focused primarily on compassionate ministry and ethnic congregations. While these continue to be important areas of concentration for those in the Wesleyan-Holiness tradition, other important methodological approaches are needed to address the additional intricacies of city centers. The urban world has become more than those who live within the city limits—it is an environment by which we are all affected, regardless of one's address.

---

12 Leigh Gallagher, *The End of the Suburbs: Where the American Dream Is Moving* (New York: Portfolio/Penguin, 2013), 14.

13 Soong-Chan Rah, *The Next Evangelicalism: Freeing the Church from Western Cultural Captivity* (Downers Grove, IL: InterVarsity Press, 2009), 126.

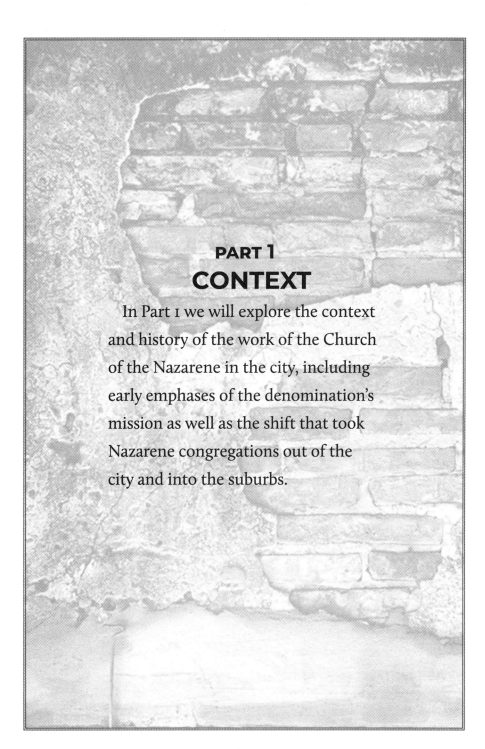

PART 1

CONTEXT

In Part 1 we will explore the context and history of the work of the Church of the Nazarene in the city, including early emphases of the denomination's mission as well as the shift that took Nazarene congregations out of the city and into the suburbs.

1

URBAN BEGINNINGS

"Neither the origin nor the subsequent history of the Church of the Nazarene can be understood without a knowledge of the two holiness traditions, urban and rural. . . . To balance them one against the other has been the task of Nazarene churchmanship ever since the union at Pilot Point in 1908."

—*Timothy L. Smith*

Early Christianity in the Greco-Roman cities of the Roman Empire was primarily an urban movement that introduced men and women, rich and poor, slave and free, to Jesus Christ. For the first hundred years, the impact of Christianity in rural areas was minimal compared to the effect in cities. In *Cities of God*, Rodney Stark demonstrates through scientific data and statistical analysis that the early rise and spread of Christianity was an urban phenomenon, accomplished through ordinary Christians living out their faith in Christian communities. He observes, "The original meaning of the word 'pagan' (*paganus*) was 'rural person,' or more colloquially 'country hick.' It came to have religious meaning because after Christianity had triumphed in the cities, most of the rural people remained unconverted."[1]

The reason for this urban emphasis was strategic. The apostle Paul was a city person whose ministry strategy, according to Stark, was focused completely on planting city churches. There is no biblical or extrabiblical record of Paul ever

---

1 Rodney Stark, *Cities of God: The Real Story of How Christianity Became an Urban Movement and Conquered Rome* (San Francisco: HarperSanFrancisco, 2006), 2.

preaching or teaching outside a city. "Pauline Christianity was entirely urban. In that respect, it stood on the growing edge of the Christian movement, for it was in the cities of the Roman Empire that Christianity, though born in the village of Palestine, had its greatest successes until well after Constantine."[2] While the contribution of missionaries like Paul was vital to the growth of early Christian communities, Stark suggests that conversions happened most often and most rapidly through the close social networks and relationships of ordinary urban Christians.

The objectives of such a concentrated focus in the cities were obvious. Cities were more densely populated than rural areas. Ramsay MacMullen estimates that the average population density in cities of the Roman Empire may have approached 200 per acre—an equivalent to modern Western cities found only in industrial slums.[3] Cities were places where political and cultural power resided, and due to the fact that they were most often the first destination of immigrants seeking a fresh start, cities were also cosmopolitan. This factor led cities to be more flexible than country hamlets, more open to change. First-century cities were linked together by Roman highways and trade routes, and became the economic engines whereby people could buy, sell, market, and trade. Urbanization became more than a choice of where one would live; it was a way to survive. Truly, "urbanization became the means of Hellenization."[4]

Within twenty years of the crucifixion and resurrection of Jesus, Christianity was transformed from a relatively small and exclusive faith in rural Galilee to an urban missionary movement reaching to the largest, most influential cultural centers in the Roman Empire. The mission of the first Christians was conceived from start to finish as an urban strategy.[5] It could be argued that the Christian faith eventually gained the attention of the broader expanse of society precisely *because* it captured the heart of the cities.

In further historical research of the early church, Rodney Stark offers a profound case for Christianity's success in the urban areas: "To cities filled with the homeless and impoverished, Christianity offered charity as well as

---

2 Wayne A. Meeks, *The First Urban Christians: The Social World of the Apostle Paul* (New Haven, CT: Yale University Press, 1983), 8.

3 Ramsay MacMullen, *Roman Social Relations: 50 B.C. to A.D. 284* (New Haven, CT: Yale University Press, 1974), 28–56.

4 Meeks, *The First Urban Christians*, 11.

5 Meeks, *The First Urban Christians*, 10.

hope. To cities filled with newcomers and strangers, Christianity offered an immediate basis for attachments. To cities filled with widows and orphans, Christianity provided a new and expanded sense of family. To cities torn by violent ethnic strife, Christianity offered a new basis for social solidarity . . . [for what Christians] brought was not simply an urban movement, but *a new culture.*"[6]

These were not the only spiritual factors at work in the first century that account for the impact of the first Christian movement, but the fact remains that any church with the goal of making Christlike disciples in the nations should go where the most potential converts can be found. This mission is not license to neglect the suburban, extra-urban, rural, or other populations, for all are in need of Christ. Nonetheless, it is necessary to underscore, and history bears it out, that "all ambitious missionary movements are, or soon become, urban."[7] While Stark's conclusions that the early success of propagating Christianity was primarily in cities, and then moved to rural areas, the vast majority of Nazarene work today is in the rural and suburban contexts. Yet that is not how the Church of the Nazarene began—it began in the city.

Phineas Bresee and the First Nazarenes

The Church of the Nazarene was born as a progeny of the Wesleyan Revival of the eighteenth century and the American Holiness Movement of the nineteenth century. From these various streams of Holiness teaching and practice, perfect love and human suffering were inextricably linked together. Holiness was both the motivation for compassion and the remedy for human misery.

Thus, holiness-minded people were inexorably drawn to the urban poor. Dissatisfied with internal dissensions, overly controlling ecclesiastical hierarchies, and controversies over doctrinal differences, Holiness leaders and laities turned their focus and energy toward those whom they deemed neglected at best, and forgotten at worst. Setting aside ecclesial boundaries, urban congregations from multiple theological backgrounds labored together to "precipitate a national Pentecost which they hoped would baptize America in the Holy Spirit and in some mystic

---

6 Stark, *Cities of God*, 162. Emphasis added.
7 Stark, *Cities of God*, 25.

manner destroy the evils of slavery, poverty, and greed."[8] Driven by postmillennial eschatology, utopian dreams for a Christian century and a national vision for "Christianizing Christianity" seemed within the grasp of Holiness churches.[9]

These parallel streams of holiness-minded churches converged in the late nineteenth century to form the National Camp Meeting Association for the Promotion of Holiness. The intermingling of Wesleyan-Arminian theology, Methodist polity, and evangelical revivalism from a variety of denominational traditions made for a curious concoction of camp-meeting-styled Wesleyanism. As a result of this unusual blend, just twenty years before the Church of the Nazarene was officially established, several distinct groups were being formed. Timothy Smith comments on these dissimilar groups' composition: "One, largely rural, was more emotionally demonstrative, emphasized rigid standards of dress and behavior, and often scorned ecclesiastical discipline. The other was urban, intellectual, and somewhat less zealous about outward standards of holiness."[10] Smith's observation cannot be understated.

When the founders of the Church of the Nazarene merged three separate denominations into one, each group originated from a different geographical region of the United States. The Association of Pentecostal Churches of America was from the east, the Holiness Church of Christ was from the south and southwest, and the Church of the Nazarene was from the west.[11] While each denomination shared common interests in the sanctified life and holiness evangelism, their other emphases were remarkably varied. "The East Coast Nazarenes worked among immigrant groups, most notably Cape Verdeans. West Coast Nazarenes reached out to inner city poor, the Japanese immigrants in the orange groves, indigenous and immigrant Mexicans, and Chinese-Americans."[12] One emphasized the sacraments and education. Another emphasized enthusiastic worship and the avoidance of worldliness. Still another emphasized social work and a desire

---

8 Timothy L. Smith, *Revivalism and Social Reform in Mid-19th-Century America* (Nashville: Abingdon Press, 1957), 62.

9 Harold E. Raser, "'Christianizing Christianity': The Holiness Movement As a Church, *the* Church, or No Church at All?" Published by the Church of the Nazarene, n.d., https://www.usacanadaregion.org/sites/usacanadaregion.org/files/Roots/Resources/Christianizing%20Christianity%20by%20Harold%20Raser.pdf.

10 Smith, *Called unto Holiness*, 435.

11 Stan Ingersol, *Past and Prospect: The Promise of Nazarene History* (Eugene, OR: Wipf and Stock, 2014), 21.

12 Ingersol, *Past and Prospect*, 10.

to build a center of holy fire that would evangelize the cities of the nation.[13] Ultimately, the early Nazarenes were attempting to weave together three separate ideological perspectives.

Because these early differences were emphatically evident, Nazarene historians document modifications of missional focus that have taken place through generational shifts over the past hundred years, particularly in relation to social change.

The first generation, those who had doggedly defended holiness during the late nineteenth century, considered Christ, to use H. Richard Niebuhr's classification, as the Transformer of culture. *The first generation's orientation was urban.* The chief early centers of the church that became Nazarene were in such cities as Brooklyn, Los Angeles, Nashville, and Glasgow. The leaders—including Bresee, Reynolds, A. M. Hills, B. F. Haynes, John T. Benson, and George Sharpe—had come out of established denominations[14] and possessed a sense of custodianship for culture. Their concerns for society were deep. They built rescue missions and homes for unwed mothers and pushed forward the temperance movement.[15]

"The second generation of Nazarenes, by contrast, was *rural* in orientation."[16] Prominent leaders during this period, such as R. T. Williams and J. B. Chapman, had an early connection with Bresee but were raised in ecclesiastical settings that were defined by the rural ethos of revivalism and camp meetings. Their perspective fit Niebuhr's classification of Christ against culture, leading to a wave of Nazarenes withdrawing from mainstream culture.

Following the path of many in post-World War II America, the third generation of Nazarenes began to move into newly created suburbs on the outskirts of declining central city cores.[17] Although more will be said about the impact of the rise of suburbia on the Church of the Nazarene's engagement with urban areas, an underlying inspiration for suburbs grew out of Victorian "ideals of domestic

---

13 Smith, *Called unto Holiness,* 52.

14 Bresee and Reynolds: Methodist Episcopal Church; Haynes and Benson: Methodist Episcopal Church, South; Sharpe: Methodist Episcopal Church, Congregationalist.

15 Floyd Cunningham, ed., Stan Ingersol, Harold E. Raser, and David P. Whitelaw, *Our Watchword and Song: The Centennial History of the Church of the Nazarene* (Kansas City, MO: Beacon Hill Press of Kansas City, 2009), 10–11. Emphasis added.

16 Cunningham et al., *Our Watchword and Song,* 11. Emphasis added. Mainline churches were located primarily in urban areas.

17 Cunningham et al., *Our Watchword and Song,* 11.

purity"[18] and as an escape from the moral entrapments of the decaying urban life. Nazarene historians have identified this era in the Church of the Nazarene as Niebuhr's classification of Christ being "*of* culture."[19]

Articulating Nazarene history through the lens of Niebuhr's classifications of how ecclesiastical bodies deal with cultural change is helpful to understanding the denomination because it stresses the missional accent of either centripetal or centrifugal flow in each generation.[20] A Christ-transforming-culture model—the primary worldview of first-generation Nazarenes—emphasizes hands-on action to reform society and human flourishing. A Christ-against-culture model—the primary worldview of second-generation Nazarenes—sees culture more negatively and tends to emphasize withdrawal from society, even to the point of creating countercultural enclaves. A Christ-*of*-culture model—the primary worldview of third-generation Nazarenes—attempts to hold the two previous approaches in balance, yet begins to move toward accommodation of civil religion. While Niebuhr did not categorize any group exclusively into one model, the distinctions are telling. Worldview determines vision; vision determines mission; mission determines strategy.

The move from the Christ-transforming model to the Christ-against-culture model represented a major shift in focus. Early Nazarenes focused their holiness evangelism and compassionate ministries in urban areas such as Boston, Los Angeles, Chicago, and Nashville. The earliest international missionary work in India and Japan centered on cities such as Calcutta (now Kolkata) and Tokyo. Conversely, the second generation of leaders had southern roots and were more aligned with revivalistic techniques, such as transportable tents with sawdust floors in small, rural towns. While the differences were not matters of right or wrong, the difference in missional strategy was dramatic. In this period, "the church shifted attention from Tokyo to Kyoto and from Calcutta to Buldana, and, in America, from the cities to the Midwestern farm belt."[21]

This shift was a significant departure from the vision of the early Nazarenes, particularly those from the American northeast and west. At the dawn of the

---

18 Harvie M. Conn and Manuel Ortiz, *Urban Ministry: The Kingdom, the City, and the People of God* (Downers Grove, IL: IVP Academic, 2001), 69–70.

19 Cunningham et al., *Our Watchword and Song*, 11. Emphasis added.

20 Centripetal flow is directed inward toward the center. Centrifugal flow is directed outward from the center.

21 Cunningham et al., *Our Watchword and Song*, 346.

twentieth century cities were growing rapidly, bringing with them the associated aspects of compact urban environments: overcrowding, unemployment, pollution, poverty, corruption, and crime.[22] While many urban congregations were escaping the cities, the Holiness associations saw these raw urban conditions as an open door to reach desperate, broken, and—in many cases—spiritually open people with the gospel.

Bresee believed the conditions were ripe for perfect love and Christlike ministry to the lowest levels of society. His disappointment with the Methodist Episcopal Church—for what he believed was a disregard for the poor and disenfranchised—prompted him to do the unthinkable: request a relocation away from a prestigious assignment to work with a rescue mission in downtown Los Angeles. There would be no return for Bresee. Even though his initial foray into the complexities and injustices of the city proved difficult, Bresee had tapped into his God-given passion and divine calling—a missional commitment of holiness evangelism to the toiling masses of the world.[23]

He did not set out to begin a church, but when Bresee and his followers officially organized themselves on October 20, 1895, they knew their providential purpose. "They professed a definite sense of divine calling. They intended to be a church, not a mission or association. They were committed to the doctrine of entire sanctification as a second definite work of divine grace. And, finally, they believed that they had a special mission to the urban poor."[24]

They would call themselves the Church of the Nazarene, associated by name and affiliation with the ministry of Jesus to the outcast, marginalized, forgotten, and displaced people of the world. Bresee and those first Nazarenes were "convinced that the *special* calling of the Church of the Nazarene was *first* to plant 'centers of holy flame' in the great cities of America."[25] The phrase "centers of holy flame" denoted a calling especially to the urban core and "wherever also may be found waste places and souls seeking pardon and cleansing from sin."[26]

---

22 "Rise of Industrial America, 1876–1900: City Life in the Late 19th Century," Library of Congress, http://www.loc.gov/teachers/classroommaterials/presentationsandactivities/presentations/timeline/riseind/city/.

23 Early Nazarenes were purposeful in their use of the word "toiling." They identified it as a descriptive symbol of Jesus's ministry to the poor and distressed of the world: "the toiling, lowly mission of Christ and [thus] the mission of Christ's followers." Cunningham et al., *Our Watchword and Song*, 101.

24 Cunningham et al., *Our Watchword and Song*, 100.

25 Cunningham et al., *Our Watchword and Song*, 107.

26 Cunningham et al., *Our Watchword and Song*, 100.

But all of that began to change, and change rapidly. Such change is the subject of the next chapter.

A Church for the City
Los Angeles First Church of the Nazarene

The church that began in 1895 in the Glory Barn of Los Angeles is still thriving today, carrying on Phineas F. Bresee's vision and legacy. In 1960, the then predominantly white congregation moved to a thriving area of the city, five miles from downtown. But by 1980, the neighborhood had begun to change drastically, and the church's leaders decided to stay and change *with* the neighborhood. In 1992 the second flashpoint of the L.A. riots happened just two blocks from the church, and a majority of businesses and homeowners left the area. When the church still stayed, it signaled to the remaining community that the congregation and its pastors really wanted to work for the well-being of the neighborhood.

Rev. Dr. Michael Mata served as part of the pastoral team from 1980 until 1997 and, after devoting himself to twenty years of urban ministry education, is now serving again as associate pastor for community engagement. In fact, the current lead pastor of the English-speaking congregation, Rev. Josue Tiguila, was a student in Mata's youth group. Mata has witnessed tremendous change in the neighborhood over the last forty years since the majority population is Latino[27] immigrants, primarily from Central America, with Korean-American residents and business owners and, now, an established Bangladeshi community.

Comprising five different language/cultural congregations, L.A. First reflects the diversity of its surroundings. Its congregations include English-speaking, Spanish-speaking, Filipino, Korean (with most having been born in Korea but raised in the U.S.), and the only North Korean congregation in the United States. Combined, these congregations currently average 350 in weekly attendance, but more than one thousand people come through the church doors on a weekly basis to receive services from congregational volunteers and collaborating partners who offer meals, nursing care, and youth development programs. As part of their commitment to being responsible for the well-being of their community, Mata

---

27 Any references to the Latino community in this book should be understood as inclusive of all, regardless of gender.

serves on the Mayor's Interfaith Task Force, which deals with issues of housing, job development, immigration, and climate change.

Looking back on these last four decades, Mata recognizes the church's commitment to shared values as what has guided them to have a consistent presence in a changing community. "We need to be 'fringe-centric,'" he said. "We have to be focused on the well-being of the people at the fringes; this is not an upward-mobile journey." With that perspective, the pastors and congregation are able to care for the well-being of the church's neighbors, regardless of where congregants live. But, in this densely populated area of the city, most congregants are neighbors, and neighbors often become congregants.

For Reflection or Discussion

1. Is there any part of the Nazarene origins story that is new or surprising to you? If so, what is it, and why?
2. Imagine if some of the founding Nazarenes moved into your city right now. In what area do you think they would start a church? What are the critical issues in your city, and which ones do you think they would give themselves to?
3. H. Richard Niebuhr offered three models for understanding the intersection of church and culture: Christ transforming culture; Christ against culture; and Christ of culture. How do you see each of these models of thought and action at work in your own church and/or city?

City Practice
Learning Your History

Do you know how and when your denomination came to your city, or to the city nearest you? If not, do some work of exploration and discovery to learn the story. The central offices for your denomination should have statistical records and other information; you can also interview elder parishioners and retired clergy in your area. Who began the work of your denomination in your city, when, and why? How has it grown and/or changed since then? If no one else has done so, write out the narrative history of the denomination for your area. Consider how your current church and/or your future plans are connected to this history, whether building on existing foundations or redeeming past mistakes.

2

THE GREAT REVERSAL

In spite of the specific urban calling so evident in its earliest days, the Church of the Nazarene, on the whole, did not remain in the cities of America. The factors that led the Church of the Nazarene to depart from a distinctive earlier commitment to social ministries in the urban context are varied, but related. These factors can be addressed by a sociological movement called the Great Reversal. This term, first coined by Timothy Smith, refers to the radical shift evangelicals made in the early twentieth century from an evangelistic social concern to an altered focus on individualistic evangelism and fundamentalist theology.[1] The earlier evangelistic social concern was interested in personal evangelism but held that personal transformation accompanied social transformation. This strongly held conviction led to the establishment of orphanages, homes for unwed mothers, city rescue missions, schools for immigrants, and the church working to support government legislation to bring about social change. However, the Great Reversal brought a significant modification: the social gospel became linked with liberal theology.

Timothy Smith's *Revivalism and Social Reform* "was one of the single most explosive theses in the history of the American Society of Church History." It was disruptive "because in 1958 it was still a foregone conclusion that if any evangelical talked about the kingdom, he was a liberal, a modernist who didn't believe the Bible, and had been taken in by German higher criticism."[2] This mindset

---

1 David O. Moberg, *The Great Reversal: Reconciling Evangelism and Social Concern* (Eugene, OR: Wipf & Stock Publishers, 2006), 11, 30.
2 Ralph D. Winter, "Understanding the Polarization between Fundamentalist and Modernist Mission," *International Journal of Frontier Missiology* 26 (Spring 2009), 6.

dominated the American evangelical mind so completely that a dichotomy formed between two types of Christianity: one that saved souls for heaven and another that worked to change earthly social structures.

In his seminal book on the Great Reversal, David Moberg argued that, with the modernist-fundamentalist debate, great revivalist preachers became soul winners, preaching that true social reform must begin with the individual, rather than with society.[3] As the liberal wing of the church dropped the responsibility of preaching the gospel, the evangelical wing felt greater pressure to fill in the gap. Further, when individualism continued to emerge as a driving ethos in greater American thinking, it was easier to associate being Christian with being American. Conservative politics became enmeshed with conservative religion. Rather than poverty being a systemic problem that must be fixed, the goals of prosperity and success grew to be the inalienable right of every person.

Soong-Chan Rah notes, "There was a time when evangelicals had a balanced position that gave proper attention to both evangelism and social concern, but a great reversal early in this [twentieth] century led to a lopsided emphasis upon evangelism and omission of most aspects of social involvement."[4] Moberg's and Smith's work reiterated that there can be no social gospel without evangelism—because welfare does not eliminate personal or spiritual emptiness. Likewise, personal evangelism that does not also address unjust and discriminating social systems fails to deal with the systemic sins of society. Evangelism and social concern go hand in hand. This principle is true to Christian faith generally, and Wesleyan roots specifically.

These cultural tensions were strongly felt among Nazarenes. As the modernist-fundamentalist controversy raged, conservative Christians, including many Methodists, felt disenfranchised from what they perceived as the liberalization of their mainline denominations. A number of these migrated to the Church of the Nazarene, bringing with them more Reformed theological positions and fundamentalist leanings. Fear became a primary reason to dissociate from a rapidly changing culture. There were perceived and real cultural dangers to confront: Communism, Darwinism, modernism, and atheism, to name a few. They felt as if the secure world they had known was disintegrating before their eyes. Even the

---

3 Moberg, *The Great Reversal*, 11, 30.
4 Soong-Chan Rah, *The Next Evangelicalism: Freeing the Church from Western Cultural Captivity* (Downers Grove, IL: InterVarsity Press, 2009), 96.

authority and veracity of the Bible were being challenged in educational institutions with newfangled ideologies like higher criticism. Cities were perceived as strong magnets for these threats to the life of faith.

Accompanying these fears were other aspects of fundamentalist theology, including a changing eschatology. Premillennialism replaced postmillennialist theology. The majority of early Nazarene leaders were postmillennial in their thinking. This more optimistic view of the *parousia*—the Christian belief in the second coming of Christ—believed that the in-breaking kingdom of God would make the world a better place, and added a sense of urgency to work for societal change to prepare the way for the return of Christ. Alternatively, premillennialist thought maintained that society would continue to deteriorate and that Christ would return only when society had reached its lowest point. For premillennialists, cities represented everything that was wrong with the world. The vice, sin, and darkness of cities appeared complex and dangerous. Urban centers were perceived as politically liberal, theologically adrift, and wildly perilous. "These rural Methodists felt alienated from urban culture. . . . Their piety and pessimism outweighed social concern. Fear colored the whole sphere of sociological change. Many Holiness people, like other Americans, became caught up in the view that there was some plot working against the basic premises and morals of Christianity."[5]

Conversely, the countryside felt conservative and safe. In response to these real and perceived threats to the moral fabric of their country,[6] Nazarenes felt obligated to make a choice. Stan Ingersol observes that American Protestantism had been effectively polarized into two different camps.[7] Denominations were asked to cast their votes, if not their lots. In the perilous environment of the cultural hurricane, it was deemed an easy choice. In 1928, at the seventh General Assembly of the Church of the Nazarene, General Superintendent R. T. Williams spoke clearly and adamantly, "First, we note with pleasure that there are no differences or divisions among us. We are a perfectly united denomination. In this General Assembly, there will be no discussions of modernism or fundamentalism. We are *all* fundamentalists. . . . Every man in

---

5 Floyd Cunningham, ed., Stan Ingersol, Harold E. Raser, and David P. Whitelaw, *Our Watchword and Song: The Centennial History of the Church of the Nazarene* (Kansas City, MO: Beacon Hill Press of Kansas City, 2009), 185.

6 The majority of Nazarenes in the 1920s and '30s lived in the United States.

7 Stan Ingersol, *Past and Prospect: The Promise of Nazarene History* (Eugene, OR: Wipf and Stock, 2014), 12. Ingersol refers to the introduction of a "two-party system" in American Protestantism.

this body is a fundamentalist. . . . A modernist would be very lonesome in this General Assembly."[8]

While Williams undoubtedly believed the fundamentals to be the authority of Scripture, the deity of Christ, and the unchanging character of God, the die had been cast. An intentional—or perhaps unintentional—choice had been made that set into motion what Nazarene historian Paul Bassett characterized as "the fundamentalist leavening of the Holiness Movement."[9] The unintended consequences of this decision created a new denominational agenda. The theological conversation for Nazarenes had changed.[10] The first leaders were gone and, with them, an ongoing concern for the plight of the urban poor. National morality was flagging, and the fear of losing holiness children was fierce. Accommodation felt like compromise. "Such a situation inevitably deepened the isolation among Nazarenes and taught them to despair of ever making the cities of America a garden of the Lord."[11] It was time to separate from worldly ways and ungodly influences. When the separation was complete, the cities of America were left behind.

If the Church of the Nazarene left the cities largely due to a fear of what they represented, and in reaction to the social gospel's deficient emphasis on evangelism, there was also the increasing influence of southern church leadership. In his historical overview of the evangelical church in the American city, Harvie Conn observes that, because urbanization came much later in the south, its primary impact leaned more toward a rural and frontier mindset. While the religious institutions in the south greatly influenced cultural ideas and mores, "unlike the north, southern revivalism had little impact on social reform." Due to the prevalence of slavery in the south, morality was restricted to more privatized areas of rural-middle-class virtues like "self-restraint, self-discipline, and the encouragement of familial and neighborly responsibilities."[12] This reality was deeply felt in the Church of the Nazarene.

---

8 R. T. Williams, "Address of the General Superintendents," *Seventh General Assembly Journal* (1928), 49. Quoted in Paul M. Bassett, "The Fundamentalist Leavening of the Holiness Movement, 1914–1940, The Church of the Nazarene: A Case Study," *Wesleyan Theological Journal* Vol. 13 (Spring 1978): 75–76.

9 Bassett, "The Fundamentalist Leavening," 65–91.

10 Ingersol, *Past and Prospect*, 12.

11 Smith, *Called unto Holiness*, 29.

12 Harvie M. Conn, *The American City and the Evangelical Church: A Historical Overview* (Grand Rapids: Baker Books, 1994), 39.

Moreover, when the first generation of Nazarene leaders faded from the scene, the second generation nurtured different passions. R. T. Williams and J. B. Chapman, the last two general superintendents with direct ties to Bresee and Pilot Point, Texas, were from the southern wing of the church. Prior to becoming a general superintendent, Chapman was editor of the denominational periodical, *Herald of Holiness* (now called *Holiness Today*). Believing the modernist-fundamentalist controversy was important to the integrity of the Church of the Nazarene, and in an effort to extend a welcoming hand to distressed fundamentalists searching for a new ecclesiastical home, Chapman revealed his bias in a 1924 editorial: "Unity was impossible between men who believed 'in . . . *a program of social and educational services* . . . and a world-wide program of Pentecostal evangelism.' Liberals might tolerate fundamentalists, but the latter could *never 'cater to the doctrines and efforts of the social reformer.'"*[13]

Another popular Nazarene leader, Reuben Robinson, emerged during this time and was affectionately called "Uncle Buddie." Born in a log cabin in the Smoky Mountains, Robinson eventually moved to Texas to be a sharecropper and ranch hand. He was radically saved during a sawdust camp meeting, and—despite his physical challenges and lack of education—became one of the most sought-after and effective evangelists in the history of the Church of the Nazarene. Williams, Chapman, and Robinson were widely respected and carried inestimable clout within the denomination, but their orientation was more agrarian and rural than cosmopolitan and urban.

Post-WWII Shifts in the Church of the Nazarene

Another denominational shift occurred after World War II. With a burgeoning economy and the introduction of the commuter lifestyle, many Nazarenes moved away from urban areas to expanding suburbs, further removing them from urban culture, particularly in the sense of regular interaction with the marginalized of society.

With this detachment came the formalizing of compassionate ministries as a programmatic arm of the church: "The fourth generation [of Nazarenes] witnessed a rapid expansion of the church on its international frontiers. By the

---

13 James Blaine Chapman, *Herald of Holiness* (November 5, 1924). Quoted in Smith, *Called unto Holiness*, 319. Emphases added.

end of this era, the Church of the Nazarene was larger outside North America than within it. . . . The era saw an emphasis upon compassionate ministries. Nazarenes held Christ and culture in paradox, at home equally in the church and the world and not always recognizing or solving the tensions this involved. . . . During the fourth generation, the Nazarene parish indeed became the world."[14] Compassionate ministries looked less and less like ministry to the urban poor in the United States and more and more like the building and resourcing of hospitals and schools internationally. It could be argued that this was merely a natural evolution of compassion—but something had changed. When the Church of the Nazarene broadened its horizons to a world parish, it became easier to neglect the neighborhood parish.

During the 1948 General Assembly of the Church of the Nazarene, General Superintendent H. V. Miller encouraged the young denomination to focus district church-planting strategies in rural areas.

> In the formative years of our denominational existence, we have wisely tried to establish our work in centers of population. The time has now come when we should face the challenge of necessity of planning for the rural areas as well. . . . We should deliberately plan as districts to evangelize the rural areas as opportunity affords. Are we fully aware that fifty percent of our population is rural? . . . It is quite likely that some legislation will be necessary to encourage districts to set up circuits where such will meet the needs of a given area.[15]

Legislation was passed, formally setting into motion what was already the trajectory of the denomination. The Church of the Nazarene would become a rural and suburban church. It seemed like a logical step, based on the waning interest in urban areas, but it turned out to be a self-fulfilling prophecy for the denomination.

The sociological and generational survey of the Church of the Nazarene explains the ebb and flow of urban ministry over the past century. However, the movement from urban to rural then suburbia to world is reflective not only of contextual processes and leadership interests in each generation but also of the

---

14 Cunningham et al., *Our Watchword and Song*, 11, 12.

15 H. V. Miller, "General Superintendents' Quadrennial Address," General Assembly of the Church of the Nazarene, 1948.

shifting tides of evangelicalism more broadly. The Church of the Nazarene has largely been swept along with the mainstream of sociological adaptation over the decades, beginning in the United States and broadening to the international stage.

Toward the Suburbs in the Church

Societal changes greatly influenced the evangelical urban strategy, with demographics being a major factor. Research indicates that Protestants began leaving urban areas as early as 1850, with many congregations changing property locations every few decades.[16] Government programs that made home purchases more accessible to white populations and facilitated the development of municipal infrastructure encouraged the movement of white people away from urban centers. Moreover, as denominations began to move away from the cities their churches began to reach a different kind of socioeconomic member—less blue collar and more middle class. This upwardly mobile trajectory and the relocation of congregations to more suburban areas had the twofold effect of (1) moving closer to primarily white middle-class members and suburban culture, and (2) moving away from primarily non-white lower-class members who could not afford to relocate.

When people lived together in the cities, the poor and the rich were neighbors. They shopped in the same stores, and their children went to the same schools. Once whites moved to the suburbs, it became easier to stigmatize those who were left in the cities.[17] Gibson Winter, a former University of Chicago Divinity School professor and social justice advocate, lived through what he described in his provocative 1961 book as "the Protestant exodus from the central city."[18] In that book, *The Suburban Captivity of the Churches*, Winter observes, "These were almost inevitable movements for religious institutions whose principle of organization is the voluntary congregation; such churches move when the [most involved] members leave the area."[19] Whether it was intended or not, these relocations were perceived by many to be abandoning the urban poor and, in so doing, forsaking the calling of the urban mission of the church.

---

16 Gibson Winter, *The Suburban Captivity of the Churches: An Analysis of Protestant Responsibility in the Expanding Metropolis* (Garden City, NY: Doubleday and Company, 1961), 42.

17 Ron Benefiel, personal email to author, October 18, 2015.

18 Winter, *The Suburban Captivity of the Churches*, 3.

19 Winter, *The Suburban Captivity of the Churches*, 47.

Nazarenes did not escape the "suburban captivity of the churches." Between 1950 and 1970, several prominent Nazarene churches moved from downtown locations to more suburban areas, including Los Angeles First Church and Chicago First Church.[20] Urban missiologist Tom Nees indicates that most Nazarene churches began as neighborhood-based congregations but quickly became family-based congregations, gradually decreasing their engagement with neighborhood needs and opportunities.[21] This meant that when families moved, the churches moved with them. The indicators that an expanding church used to measure impact and growth no longer fit the models needed to be effective in the urban environment.[22]

While some of these changes were based on class differences, the relocations were also racially motivated. After a century of slavery in America and the lowest-possible wages for sharecroppers and other hard-labor jobs, black Americans became an unnecessary labor force in the southern economy. The mechanical cotton picker became functional in the mid-1940s, immediately replacing forty field laborers. By the end of World War II, the vast majority of manual laborers were redundant. Millions of people from the south were instantly unemployed and displaced. The jobs were in the industrialized north, almost exclusively in large cities. This event became known as the Second Great Migration.[23] "Black Americans moved from the South to the North; five million of them moved after 1940, during the time of the mechanization of cotton farming. In 1970, when the migration ended, black America was only half Southern, and less than a quarter rural; 'urban' had become a euphemism for 'black.' The black migration was one of the largest and most rapid mass internal movements of people in history—perhaps the greatest not caused by immediate threat of execution or starvation."[24]

The social impact of this migration has been well documented. However, at the time the migration was taking place, few people seemed to be asking the fun-

---

20 Cunningham et al., *Our Watchword and Song*, 435.

21 Tom Nees, personal email to author, October 7, 2015.

22 Jim Copple, personal email to author, October 12, 2015.

23 The First Great Migration (1910–1930) witnessed more than one million people move from the rural south to the urban northeast and midwest. The Second Great Migration, following the Great Depression and continuing until the middle of the Vietnam War (1940–1970), saw another five million people flood to the urban areas of the northeast and California.

24 Nicholas Lemann, *The Promised Land: The Great Black Migration and How It Changed America* (New York: Vintage Books, 1992). Quoted in Glen Kehrein, "The Times They Are a-Changing: The Suburbanization of Poverty," in *A Heart for the Community: New Models for Urban and Suburban Ministry*, eds. John Fuder and Noel Castellanos (Chicago: Moody Publishers, 2013), 298.

damental questions of where five million dislocated people would live, how they would be integrated into dramatically different cultures, and how they would be employed and educated. Although Jim Crow laws no longer applied, racism was rampant. The urban world exploded into flames that no one knew how to contain. "Resistance to blacks moving into white communities preceded a wholesale exodus, often referred to as 'white flight,' and resulted in the transformation of most major cities."[25] While it was obvious that African Americans needed to live somewhere, many people did not want them to live next door. Entire black communities were forced into ghettos and high-rise projects. Meanwhile, European immigrants in northern cities had lived in isolated ethnic neighborhoods for decades. Entire sections of town were named for their constituents: Little Italy, Germantown, and Southies in Boston. They were cities within cities. But, while these Europeans were immigrants, they were *white* immigrants.

White flight was not only a residential phenomenon; urban church congregations soon followed suit. Gibson Winter's observations regarding the immigration of European whites and African Americans to urban areas were revealing and predictive:

> The in-migration of White and Negro [sic] newcomers also had a special effect; the Protestant retreat from these newcomers has created a schism in metropolitan religious life; the major White denominations[26] are retreating to the suburban and satellite areas, while Negro [sic] and sectarian Protestantism are beginning to dominate central city areas. The major White denominations have moved toward exclusive identification with the White middle-classes; in fact, they are insulating themselves geographically from the working-class people of the metropolitan areas. The net effect of population change has been an upgrading of the major denominations through social and physical insulation from the working classes.[27]

---

25 Kehrein, "The Times They Are a-Changing," 302.

26 The Church of the Nazarene in this time period can be described as a "white" denomination. "Cheryl Sanders, a Church of God (Anderson) scholar and pastor, included the Church of the Nazarene among the 'basically lily-white, middle-class, holiness groups reflecting the sin and shame of Racist America.'" Cheryl J. Sanders, *Saints in Exile: The Holiness-Pentecostal Experience in African American Religion and Culture* (New York: Oxford University Press, 1996), 103. Quoted in Cunningham et al., *Our Watchword and Song*, 375.

27 Winter, *The Suburban Captivity of the Churches*, 47–48.

The Church of the Nazarene was not exempt from the impact of the Second Great Migration. Thousands of African Americans migrated to Kansas City, Missouri, where the Church of the Nazarene's denominational headquarters was located. Living in one of the most segregated cities in the Midwest in the early 1940s, African Americans in Kansas City were not allowed to eat in public restaurants (only at stand-up counters in drugstores), attend theater showings, or occupy hotel rooms. Property contracts included clauses prohibiting black residents from being owners *or* tenants. "In 1940, over ninety percent of Kansas City's African-Americans lived in an area of the city bounded, from north to south, by Independence Avenue and 27th Street."[28]

The Nazarene headquarters, publishing house, and seminary were all located in that corridor. Due to overcrowded offices and changing demographics, a commission was appointed to study the issue and bring a report to the 1948 General Assembly. The commission's recommendation was to move all denominational properties to a "safer" part of town. A portion of the report stated: "We are realistically facing the fact that a strong Negro [sic] population in a community develops problems and situations that are not conducive to the best interests of work such as ours, and for which we are not justified in taking responsibility."[29] The warning was heeded, the report accepted, and the recommendation adopted. Not long thereafter, new property was acquired several miles away in what was considered to be a more desirable part of town, thus reinforcing the Great Reversal.

Toward the Suburbs in Greater American Society

Other sociological factors were at work to create modern suburbia. Housing was desperately needed to accommodate thousands of war veterans. Favorable mortgage loans made housing more affordable, and most new construction happened at the edge of city limits or beyond. Glen Kehrein notes, "In the first fifteen years after the end of World War II, 688,222 new homes were built in the Chicago metropolitan area, located either in the suburbs or the farthest reaches of the city."[30]

---

28 Cunningham et al., *Our Watchword and Song*, 368.

29 *Journal of the Twelfth General Assembly of the Church of the Nazarene*, eds. S. T. Ludwig and Greta Hamsher (n.p. [1948]), 61. Quoted in Cunningham et al., *Our Watchword and Song*, 368.

30 Kehrein, "The Times They Are a-Changing," 303.

The availability of new modes of transportation also impacted the growing of suburbia. Sean Benesh suggests that the advent of the automobile, coupled with its affordability for the average consumer, allowed middle-class people to escape the cities. "It is not an overstatement to say that the personal automobile changed the entire American culture."[31] This idea is further reinforced by urban sociologist William Flanagan: "In the ten years from 1905 to 1915, the number of registered automobiles [nationally] increased from 8,000 to 2.3 million. By 1925 there were 17.5 million; by 1930, 23 million."[32]

As America was steadily becoming a more suburban society, Ross Douthat notes that the religious community that had been so important to incarnational ministry became harder to sustain in a commuter world than it had been when small towns and urban neighborhoods were the norm.[33] Douthat further cites Dean Hoge's comprehensive study of mainline churches during that era. A representative sample of baby boomer Protestants revealed that 50 percent lived more than a hundred miles from the church where they had been confirmed and discipled.[34] Also idealized in sitcoms like *Leave It to Beaver* and *My Three Sons*, suburbanization became associated with the American dream, family values, and the middle-class good life.[35] Suburbs were close enough to the city to access the amenities the urban world provided, while being far enough away to avoid the daily struggles of life in high-density neighborhoods.

Reversing the Great Reversal

Just as the exodus to the suburbs seemed to have reached its apex, there was a small but growing evangelical resurgence back to American cities in the late 1960s, which included a remnant of Nazarenes. "Influenced by the Civil Rights

---

31 Sean Benesh, *Exegeting the City: What You Need to Know about Church Planting in the City Today* (Portland: Urban Loft Publishers, 2015), Kindle Location 793.

32 William G. Flanagan, *Urban Sociology: Images and Structure*, 5th ed. (Lanham, MD: Rowman & Littlefield Publishers, 2010), 213.

33 Ross Douthat, *Bad Religion: How We Became a Nation of Heretics* (New York: Free Press, 2012), 80.

34 Dean R. Hoge, Benton Johnson, and Donald A. Luidens, *Vanishing Boundaries: The Religion of Mainline Protestant Baby Boomers* (Louisville: Westminster John Knox Press, 1994). Quoted in Douthat, *Bad Religion*, 80.

35 *Leave It to Beaver* aired from 1957 to 1963. *My Three Sons* aired from 1960 to 1972. Later sitcoms like *Happy Days* (aired from 1974 to 1984) further perpetuated the romanticized life of suburban society. During this same period, *Good Times* (aired 1974 to 1979) highlighted an African-American family living in a high-rise project in Chicago as an alternative to suburban utopia.

movement, the desire for a holistic gospel that combined social action with evangelism, and by a growing body of theological literature that took seriously the city as a place of Christian ministry, Nazarenes joined other evangelicals in reclaiming ministry in the urban context. Nazarenes did not travel this path alone; they traveled it with other evangelicals."[36] Though many Nazarene churches were traveling the broader evangelical path to evacuate the urban centers, other internal influences began to emerge in Nazarene circles to call the church back to its roots. William Greathouse was elected president of Nazarene Theological Seminary in 1968. Greathouse's considerable influence helped reignite a passion among young, emerging pastors and church planters for the biblical and Wesleyan roots of Nazarene theology.

Greathouse was elected general superintendent for the Church of the Nazarene in 1976, but before he left the seminary, he hired a gifted and forward-thinking theologian, Mildred Bangs Wynkoop. Ordained in the Church of the Nazarene, Wynkoop had been the founding president of Japan Nazarene Theological Seminary, and taught missions and theology at Trevecca Nazarene College in Nashville. She became the theologian-in-residence at Nazarene Theological Seminary. Together, Greathouse and Wynkoop became two of the leading theological voices of the Church of the Nazarene during this important era of the church's history. Wynkoop wrote two highly influential books that inspired a renewed interest for social ministries in the urban context, *John Wesley: Christian Revolutionary* (1970) and *A Theology of Love: The Dynamic of Wesleyanism* (1972). These persuasive voices and cogent texts combined to provide a counterbalance to the fundamentalist leanings that had resulted in the Great Reversal.

Younger Nazarene pastors were listening, including Tom Nees. Pastoring in the urban core of Washington, DC, Nees confessed he was "struggling to find a way to minister to the poor of [his] city."[37] With a clearly articulated calling from God to conjoin evangelistic passion and compassionate love, Nees could see that the greatest problems of the city were deeply embedded and systemic, and required more than isolated individual renewal if real change were to occur. Like Wesley, Booth, Palmer, and Bresee before him, Nees believed that evangelical

---

36 Ingersol, *Past and Prospect*, 15.

37 Tom Nees, "Taking Holiness to the Streets," *Holiness Today* (January 2004), 30–31. Quoted in Cunningham et al., *Our Watchword and Song*, 584.

social action was necessary. "The youth movement of the 1960s, coupled with the Wesleyan renaissance and . . . the book *John Wesley: Christian Revolutionary*, by Mildred Wynkoop, reinforced in Nees the desire to see the Church of the Nazarene actively involved in society."[38]

Nees wrote a doctoral thesis in 1976 titled *The Holiness Social Ethic and Nazarene Urban Ministry*. He argued that Holiness churches represent a significant ethical tradition that is needed to motivate the whole church to respond to the social evils of society. "It is only within the relatively recent past, and then without a conscious effort to repudiate what can be referred to as the holiness social ethic, that Wesleyanism, or the Holiness Movement, has been divorced from social action. The causes for this retreat from a social ethic are many and complex, but due in part, if not primarily, to a failure to understand the ethical tradition which began with Wesley."[39]

Compelled to action, Nees founded Community of Hope, an urban-development project in the core of Washington, DC. There the gospel was proclaimed as marginalized people received health care, housing assistance, job training, legal aid, food, and clothing. A new watchword was popularized in the Church of the Nazarene: *compassionate evangelism*.

Other bright lights began to appear as Nazarenes returned to the cities with a renewed focus on ministries of mercy: The Lamb's Church in Manhattan; Golden Gate Ministries in San Francisco; Los Angeles First Church of the Nazarene (including the Bresee Institute, an experiential, intern-based program designed to expose young leaders to holistic urban ministry, led by Ron Benefiel); Shepherd Community Center in Indianapolis; Liberation Community in Fort Worth. More urban leaders soon followed: JoeAnn Ballard, David Best, John Calhoun, Seymour Cole, Dean Cowles, John Hay, Orville Jenkins, Jr., Michael Mata, Samuel Smith, Bryan Stone, Fletcher Tink, and others. The services these urban churches provided included "medical clinics for the homeless, crisis intervention, client advocacy programs, job counseling, placement, and work skill training, and halfway house residencies."[40]

---

38 Cunningham et al., *Our Watchword and Song*, 584.

39 Tom Nees, *The Holiness Social Ethic and Nazarene Urban Ministry*, doctoral thesis (Wesley Theological Seminary, 1976), 6.

40 Michael J. Christensen, *City Streets, City People: A Call for Compassion* (Nashville: Abingdon Press, 1988). Quoted in Conn, *The American City and the Evangelical Church*, 155.

The Board of General Superintendents for the Church of the Nazarene issued a proclamation in the December 1981 *Herald of Holiness* (now *Holiness Today*): "Where Christian holiness is truly alive, compassion is its beautiful fruit. . . . [Nazarenes should be always] seeking to do good to the bodies and souls of [humanity]; feeding the hungry, clothing the naked, visiting the sick and the imprisoned, and ministering to the needy, as opportunity and ability are given."[41] This proclamation was followed by a pastoral letter issued by the Board of General Superintendents in 1983, which affirmed: "A new social consciousness has moved across our church. [The] sense of 'holy compassion' was an authentic expression of the American Holiness Movement's roots in the Wesleyan Revival. The ministry of compassion was emphasized in such a manner as to place it *very near to the center of the fundamental reason for the church's existence*." The pastoral letter concluded: "In light of the biblical perspective as well as our distinctive mission . . . [such social ministries should be] incorporated in the total program of evangelism . . . to the entire community [without exclusion of people from lower socioeconomic levels]."[42]

During this period, the Church of the Nazarene formally established two urban-focused initiatives: (1) The Office of Urban Missions in 1979 and (2) Thrust to the Cities,[43] launched at the 1985 General Assembly. Led by General Superintendents Lewis, Johnson, Jenkins, Strickland, Stowe, and Greathouse, denominational leaders were supportive of and encouraged this renewed emphasis on compassionate evangelism in the cities. The tide of the Great Reversal was temporarily stemmed—but not completely contained.

---

41 Board of General Superintendents, "Proclamation," *Herald of Holiness* (December 1, 1981), 5, repeated in a similar "Proclamation," *Herald of Holiness* (November 15, 1984), 5. Quoted in Cunningham et al., *Our Watchword and Song*, 586–87.

42 Quoted in Cunningham et al., *Our Watchword and Song*, 587. Emphasis added.

43 Tom Nees, personal email to author, October 2015. The results of the Thrust to the Cities initiative were mixed. Nees comments via personal email, "I don't know of any formal 'after-action review' of the Thrust. Soon after I joined the United States/Canada office we did an informal study of the effectiveness of the Thrust in the targeted United States and Canadian cities. It might be worthwhile to interview some of those directly involved and convene an 'after-action review' committee to help the [Board of General Superintendents] learn from its efforts."

A Church for the City
Nueva Luz Urban Resource Center &
Garfield Heights (Ohio) Church of the Nazarene

In 1998 Rev. Max Rodas was pastoring in the Cleveland suburb of Medina, Ohio, when he was first confronted with the reality of the HIV/AIDS epidemic ravaging entire urban neighborhoods. The effects of the disease had begun to ripple out into Latino and African-American communities, creating a problem treatment centers weren't prepared for. Many of these new patients were not comfortable receiving care from centers that had largely been focused on the gay community up to that point. Nueva Luz Urban Resource Center was established in 1999 in the Cudell neighborhood, the hardest-hit area for HIV infections in all of Cuyahoga County.

Nueva Luz began offering HIV testing, counseling, and treatment in a church building shared with a Spanish-speaking Nazarene congregation. Not long into the project, Rodas fully relocated from the suburbs into the city and found his full-time vocational work as executive director of Nueva Luz. Even now, when given the opportunity to speak to the neighborhood, he always begins by saying, "Thank you for allowing us to live in your neighborhood with you."

Twenty years later, the organization continues to provide medical case management to ensure that every person living with HIV has a doctor and is taking medication. But they also have programs to help with housing needs, nutrition, legal services, recovery, and workforce development. In hearing the stories of their neighbors, Rodas and his team discovered that all of these issues are connected, and all of them are contributors to the cycle of poverty at work in neighborhoods like Cudell. Through these services, Nueva Luz serves an average of seven hundred individuals each month.

In 2013 Rodas was asked to be a guest preacher at a small church on the opposite side of Cleveland, in Garfield Heights. He was not expecting the twenty-person white congregation situated in a mostly African-American neighborhood to invite a Guatemalan-born pastor to lead their church. When they did, he immediately declined the invitation and began the drive back across town. But as he drove from the black and Jewish neighborhoods of Cleveland's east side into the Latino neighborhoods of Cleveland's west side, he recognized the unmistakable presence of God in his car. Rodas felt God lamenting the deep divisions in the city and the church and heard God inviting him to be part of breaking down barriers.

For the past seven years, Rodas has been serving as both pastor of Garfield Heights Church of the Nazarene and executive director of Nueva Luz. There are now significant relationships that tie the two ministries and their neighborhoods together, and the congregation looks significantly more like its surrounding neighborhood, full of racial, ethnic, and linguistic diversity. Pastor Rodas only points to the power of the Holy Spirit as he says, "I don't know why I've been chosen to be in the middle of all of this."

In his book *Prophetic Imagination,* Walter Brueggemann says that the work of the prophet is both to energize hope in the people and offer prophetic critique to systems of injustice. Rodas is well positioned to do both, and he does so with his words and his actions. "We as the church need to repent from our racism and intellectualism and wealth," he says. "We need to go back to the heart of the city."

For Reflection or Discussion

1. What emotions stirred in you as you read this chapter? Pay attention to whatever feels negative or uncomfortable; don't dismiss it too quickly. After you identify your own feelings and thoughts regarding this portion of history, take time to pray. How might the Spirit invite you to respond?
2. In this chapter Busic says, "When the church broadened its horizons to a world parish, it became easier to neglect the neighborhood parish." How have you witnessed global mission hindering local mission? How should the two be in balance?
3. What is the difference between family-based and neighborhood-based ministries? Which focus is most prevalent in your own church right now? Which has been most prevalent in your experience of past churches?

City Practice 1
Learning Your History

Spend time getting to know the racial, educational, and economic history of your city. Research current demographics and notice the differences between neighborhoods and/or sections of the city. What policies and/or events led to the current reality? How do you see the effects of white flight in your area?

City Practice 2
Learning from the Steadfast Churches

Identify churches in your city that have remained in the urban core. In most cities, these will often be congregations of color. Prayerfully consider which of these congregations you may be invited to pray for, visit, and learn from. Set up an appointment with a pastor and/or join them for worship. Position yourself with humility as a learner, recognizing the years of faithful and difficult work these congregations have been doing. Ask the Spirit to guide you into friendship and partnership.

PART 2
THEOLOGY

In Part 2 we will examine the theological foundation of Wesleyan-Holiness spirituality and ecclesiology, concentrating on the importance of small groups, the means of grace, and compassion in the formation of Christian character, as well as imagining the implications of Isaiah's vision for Christian community.

3

A WESLEYAN-HOLINESS SPIRITUALITY FOR THE CITY

The phrase "Wesleyan-Holiness" in this chapter's title is intentional. While the Wesleyan and Holiness theological perspectives are similar, they are not identical. Primitive Wesleyanism—with the resultant Wesleyan Revival of the eighteenth century—and the American Holiness Movement of the nineteenth century are distinct, not only because they originate from different centuries but also because they were born out of unique contexts.

The Wesleyan Revival arose in the context of the dawn of the industrial age in a somewhat sophisticated, if not spiritually cold, English Anglicanism, and then moved with impassioned spiritual force to the marginalized of England's society, including prisoners, coal miners, and the urban poor. The American Holiness Movement was engendered in the context of American Methodism, frontier revivalism, and the upsurge of camp meeting associations sweeping the young nation with such force that church historians have deemed this period the Second Great Awakening.[1]

Wesleyan-Holiness spirituality affirms the unique differences between these two movements, but when conjoined, they form the stream that feeds the theological foundations and collective experience of the Church of the Nazarene.

---

1 Historians date the Second Great Awakening between 1790 and 1840.

Thus, the Church of the Nazarene is not the byproduct of either one or the other; it is the result of both—an integrated offspring of each individual movement.

Urban Wesleyanism

The majority of urban church models are theologically Reformed[2] or Charismatic[3] in nature. These church-planting movements are indispensable and should be celebrated; however, a Wesleyan-Holiness voice is also needed in planting, developing, and renewing urban churches. Wesleyan practices conducive to life in the urban context focus less on theological systems and proposition-based apologetics and more on the Spirit-led vitality of what Wesley contemporaries often called "religion of the heart,"[4] a concept Don Thorsen maintains is "too categorically unsystematic and Spirit-oriented for Calvinists."[5] It is often implied that Wesleyan spirituality is more helpful in guiding the practical application of Christian discipleship, while Reformed spirituality focuses more on the propositional and logically constructed systems of belief. While this dichotomy may be exaggerated, the complexity and unpredictability of life in the city can make more technical theological constructs and inflexible institutional structures difficult to manage.

Thorsen further points out that Wesleyan spirituality serves as a deterrent to the potential danger of triumphalism often found in Pentecostalism. Wesley's strong advocacy for the poor was not based merely on compassion; it was his belief that ministry to and among the poor was also a means of God's grace to the church. The Wesleyan understanding of the means of grace—both instituted and prudential—as the channels whereby God seeks, saves, and sanctifies are potentially highly effective ways of discipling in the urban context. Acts of piety and acts of mercy are given balanced importance in Wesleyan spirituality. Prudential means of grace—such as acts of mercy and serving the poor—are as

---

2 Leading Reformed church-planting movements, led by new Calvinist theologians, include Acts 29 Network, the Gospel Coalition, and Redeemer City to City.

3 The most prominent Charismatic urban church-planting network is Hillsong Church, out of Australia. Originally affiliated with the Australian branch of the Assemblies of God, called Australian Christian Churches, Hillsong separated from them in 2018 and now consider themselves their own denomination. Hillsong Church currently has a presence in the major cities of twenty-three countries.

4 David Hempton, *Methodism: Empire of the Spirit* (New Haven, CT: Yale University Press, 2005), 204.

5 Don Thorsen, *Calvin vs. Wesley: Bringing Belief in Line with Practice* (Nashville: Abingdon Press, 2013), xv.

important to Wesleyan spiritual formation as the instituted means of grace, such as prayer, Bible study, sacraments, and Christian conferencing (or what, today, we call small groups).[6]

Wesleyanism at its core is dynamic, creative, and adaptable.[7] Adaptability is helpful in regard to being purposeful and relevant to one's context, but it does not always lend itself to reproducible models. Thus, the paradigm of Wesleyan spirituality will serve more as a toolbox than as a replicable prototype for urban churches.

Wesley's driving theological and pastoral concern was that God's grace is both saving and enabling, working with human response in synergistic ways to empower God's people for spiritual formation and redemptive work in the world. While the precision of his theological construct may be viewed as insufficient to his ecclesial practice, Wesley drew generously from the work of other theological traditions. Wesleyan scholar Randy Maddox exhibits the broad range of Wesley's generous orthodoxy by demonstrating how he integrated the traditions of Eastern and Western Christian streams of thought into a practical guide for the spiritual formation of the Methodist people. Wesley's theological construct was built on two co-definitive truths of Christianity: "Without God's grace, there is no salvation; without human participation, God's grace will not save."[8] Maddox encapsulates these parallel truths in his coined phrase "responsible grace." God's grace of free salvation is a gracious gift that no human being can earn or deserve. This is the theological understanding of *monergism*, the idea that God acts with sovereign action irrespective of human response. However, God's gracious work *also* includes an empowerment that enables every person to willfully and purposefully act in responsible obedience. This is the theological understanding of *synergism*, or the moral freedom to work with and for God's redemptive purposes for the world.

Timothy Tennent submits that "Maddox's phrase 'responsible grace' manages to capture in a single phrase the perfect balance between Augustinian pessimism and Pelagian optimism."[9] Or, said another way, without God there is no hope for

---

6 Thorsen, *Calvin vs. Wesley*, 55. John Wesley's understanding of the means of grace will be further explored in chapter 4.

7 Thorsen, *Calvin vs. Wesley*, 105, 116, 121.

8 Randy Maddox, *Responsible Grace: John Wesley's Practical Theology* (Nashville: Abingdon Press, 1994), 19.

9 Timothy Tennent, "Responsible Grace," blog, February 5, 2015, https://timothytennent.com/2015/02/05/responsible-grace-randy-maddox/.

salvation or healing, and without human response back toward God, there is no church. God's grace is part and parcel of the invitation, personally and corporately, to do God's work in the world. While salvation is always a response to the divine non-coercive initiative, the Christian's "response-ability" is indispensable. . God's prevenient, saving, sanctifying, and enabling grace continues to nourish the believer.

Maddox's contribution to Wesley studies is considerable, but none is more notable than his stress on Wesley's recognition of the human tendency toward self-justification. "Given the subtleness and deceitfulness of sin, Wesley was convinced that every Christian needed spiritual direction to provide accountability for their growth in holiness."[10] Accountability is to suggest that some form of self-imposed discipline is necessary for Christian life and witness. This personal and corporate responsibility toward growth in holiness is of particular importance to urban spirituality. In the context of overwhelming density and intricate diversity, inhabitants of cities seek interdependent relationships as a means of survival. The Wesleyan emphasis on the necessity of accountability for balanced spiritual growth is beneficial to any spirituality for the city.

Wesley was convinced that the development of Christian character and the forming of a Christian mind must be nurtured by the means of grace. This conviction was a primary reason Wesley encouraged the general rules of Methodist discipline to include the threefold injunction to avoid all known sin, to do as much good as one can, and to *attend all the ordinances of God*. These rules did not earn one God's favor but were needed to "nurture the reshaping of their character into Christlikeness."[11]

The means of grace known as Christian conferencing took on a practical component through group gatherings that included class meetings, bands, and select groups designed to encourage every person toward Christlikeness. Each of these gatherings had varying levels and depths of accountability. Small groups developed the life of the Spirit in the participants and were a means through which God extended enabling grace to each person. Without this accountability, Wesley believed that one's growth in grace was severely diminished, and he "repeatedly denounced the folly of those who desire 'the end without the means,' i.e., those who expect growth in faith and holiness without regular participation in

---

10 Maddox, *Responsible Grace*, 212.
11 Maddox, *Responsible Grace*, 25, 211, 212. Emphasis added.

the means through which God has chosen to convey grace."[12] Wesley's theological concerns for responsible grace provided a clear ecclesial structure to the Methodist movement and offers a helpful paradigm for establishing Wesleyan-Holiness churches in the urban context today.

By Maddox's own admission, adopting Wesley as a spiritual mentor does not serve current contexts well by simply duplicating his structures. Wesley's methodology fit his contemporary context and was developed in response to his specific cultural milieu. The Methodist plan of discipleship described in the general rules found practical expression in his day through the accountability of class meetings, bands, select groups, and other participation in the means of grace. Whatever form Wesleyan-Holiness spirituality takes today, finding ways to increase mutual accountability remains essential to spiritual formation. Any efforts toward planting, developing, or renewing urban churches will be dependent on returning to the Wesleyan way of personal transformation in and through Christian community. Regardless of form, the critical question of Christian conferencing—"How goes it with your soul?"[13]—finds new expression as a means of grace today.

A Church for the City
Mission New York (Harlem, New York City)

Rev. Dr. Bruce Barnard is dedicated to helping the church thrive in New York City. In his role as executive director of the Manhattan Initiative, he sees the big picture of property acquisition and development. The Manhattan Initiative oversees long-term investments for the Metro New York District of the Church of the Nazarene, and infuses funds into church planting, clergy development, and partnerships between churches and businesses. In this work, Barnard knows firsthand that the significant cost of acquiring, developing, and maintaining property in New York City can be prohibitive for new churches—which is one of the reasons he pastors a church that meets weekly in his family's apartment.

Each week the small congregation gathers together to share a meal as part of their worship service, which also includes singing, teaching, discussion, prayer,

---

12 Maddox, *Responsible Grace*, 196.
13 Henry H. Knight III and F. Douglas Powe, Jr., *Transforming Community: The Wesleyan Way to Missional Congregations* (Nashville: Discipleship Resources, 2016), Kindle Location 798.

and the Eucharist. The relationships formed in this intimate setting are a means of grace for those involved as they learn from one another, trust one another, and share their needs and experiences together. It's a church and a small group rolled into one.

A self-described "living room church," the congregation has had to change living rooms more than once since launching in 2013. But this is a normal part of life for most people living in major cities, and the gathering space is more about the people in it than its location. The makeup of the congregation has changed in that time as well, as people have moved away and newcomers have been welcomed.

There are a lot of advantages to a house church in Harlem—a densely populated and highly transitional part of the city—perhaps the most obvious being that the congregation has free space in which to worship. But even greater, Barnard says, is the opportunity to develop relationships with one's neighbors. The twelve people who gather weekly as part of Mission New York are involved and invested in one another's lives in significant ways.

"This is not a model that many would consider 'successful' in terms of numbers," Barnard admits. "But I don't think that's the only way to measure success." The congregation is working out together what it means to follow Jesus faithfully in the midst of their lives in the city, finding rich encouragement and accountability in the process. The people of Mission New York receive blessing from one another and from the city they inhabit, and they pray that, together, they are a blessing to their city as well.

For Reflection or Discussion

1. Would you previously have considered small groups (or other kinds of "Christian conferencing") as integral to Wesleyan-Holiness spirituality? Why or why not?

2. When have you been a part of a group that focused on questions like, "How goes it with your soul?" How was that group a means of grace to you? What transformation did you witness in yourself and/or others in the group?

3. In your experience (whether good or bad), what is necessary to formulate these kinds of groups, and what do they need on an ongoing basis to meet their intended purpose?

4. Developing long-term relationships around a shared desire for discipleship is essential in Wesleyan-Holiness churches, whether urban elsewhere. With this in mind, what are the immediate implications for your own church, or for your church-planting plans?

City Practice
Join a Third Place

The people in your city may not be finding community in church, but they are looking for it somewhere. A "third place" is a place of connection, community, and belonging that is not home or work. In your area, where do people gather to talk about their lives, develop friendships, and engage in projects together? These kinds of communities can be found in parks, coffee shops, gyms, volunteer organizations, or hobby clubs. Once you have identified a few of these groups, consider which one fits best with your own interests, and then join it. Allow the rhythms of the community to instruct you, and receive the grace of friendship. Be patient as the Spirit guides conversation and relationships; you are there to learn, to listen, and to notice what God is already doing.

4

URBAN ECCLESIOLOGY

Following their spiritual heritage in the Wesleyan Revival of the eighteenth century, Holiness churches in the United States—prior to and shortly following the American Civil War—were social activists with a holistic concern for personal salvation, compassionate evangelism, and biblical justice. Contrary to the notion that the revivalism of the American Holiness Movement of the nineteenth century impeded social change, Timothy Smith's doctoral thesis, *Popular Protestantism in Mid-Nineteenth-Century America*, demonstrated that the antebellum Methodists and other evangelical Holiness churches initiated and led compassionate and corporate reforms with purposeful optimism.[1]

In the spirit of the preaching and teaching of new-school Calvinists such as Asa Mahan and Charles Finney from the Oberlin Holiness revivals, the perfectionists led abolitionist campaigns and emphasized the civil rights of women and minorities. Later, leaders like Phoebe Palmer, Nathan Bangs, and Benjamin T. Roberts of the Methodist Church North emphasized a Christian perfection that underscored ministry to the urban poor in the largest cities of the northeastern United States. The dual-focused emphases of purposeful compassion and the radical optimism of personal and societal transformation helped shape an ecclesiology that remains conducive to ministry in a variety of urban environments.

A coherent ecclesiology of the city draws upon the best thinking from all Christian traditions to maximize ministry in the complexities of urban life. Ec-

---

1 Timothy L. Smith, *Popular Protestantism in Mid-Nineteenth-Century America*, PhD dissertation, Harvard University, 1955. The word "antebellum" here refers to the period of American history prior to the Civil War.

umenical diversity should not be perceived as a weakness; rather, every faithful tradition may offer a perspective that helps the whole to think and act more holistically and more holy. In his sermon "Catholic Spirit," Wesley acknowledged the limitation of an individual's worldview and championed the importance of an ecumenical approach that values the contributions of the whole: "And it is certain, so long as we know but in part, that all men will not see all things alike. It is an unavoidable consequence of the present weakness and shortness of human understanding, that several men will be of several minds in religion as well as in common life. So it has been from the beginning of the world, and so it will be 'till the restitution of all things.'"[2]

In the spirit of ecumenical thinking, scholar Don Thorsen promotes a clearly articulated Wesleyan ecclesiology, with particular attention to how the beliefs and practices of a Wesleyan viewpoint inform other predominant theological traditions. Thorsen affirms "practical divinities" that the Wesleyan tradition has contributed to the greater evangelical church and underscores Wesleyan characteristics that impact the whole of Christendom. These will be highlighted in the remainder of the chapter as Wesleyan-Holiness distinctives that shape a robust urban ecclesiology. The term "distinctives," of course, does not imply that these ecclesial qualities do not exist in other theological traditions but simply that they rise to a level of special importance and prominence in Wesleyan-Holiness teaching and application. It should also be noted that these distinctives serve the dual purpose of spiritual discipleship into the likeness of Christ.

The Optimism of Grace

Grace is a hallmark for all Christian faith—Catholic, Protestant, and Orthodox—but the immediate and ongoing impacts of grace on a person's life are expressed to varying degrees. Wesleyan-Holiness theology conveys grace, individually and corporately, with great optimism and salvific effect. Nazarenes believe that grace is needed by all and available to all irrespective of moral or social condition. Wesley was fond of portraying grace as "free for all and free in

---

2 John Wesley, "Sermon 39: Catholic Spirit," c. 1749/1750, http://wesley.nnu.edu/john-wesley/the-sermons-of-john-wesley-1872-edition/sermon-39-catholic-spirit/. Copyright 1999 by the Wesley Center for Applied Theology. For Wesley, the word "catholic" does not refer to a specific denomination or group of Christians. Rather, the term refers to the entire church, the body of Christ, as a universal fellowship of all times and all places.

all." Free *for* all means it is available to everyone; free *in* all means that grace need not be desired or even asked for.[3] It is simply available, freely given and distributed without measure, in every person. The fundamental belief in genuine, life-changing conversion that leads to radical spiritual transformation permeated the teaching, preaching, and practice of the American Holiness Movement and the early Nazarenes. "Theology infused with a personal experience of God's grace—this is Wesleyanism."[4]

The optimism of grace has a clear *telos* (meaning goal, or end). Timothy Smith affirmed that Wesley and his theological descendants professed that the pursuit of a Christlike character was the final disposition of God's grace in a person's life: "Though never implying freedom from ignorance, error, or physical or psychic frailty, [Wesley] believed hallowing grace to be available 'now, and by simple faith.' The experience of the new birth broke one free of sinful deeds and habits. The subsequent experience of 'entire' sanctification brought deliverance from the inward bent to sinning and enthroned love as the ruling impulse of the heart. . . . Nazarenes believe the original emphasis to be both scriptural and relevant."[5]

The optimism of grace extends beyond the transformation of individuals; it transforms neighborhoods, cities, and cultures. When crafting the core values for the Church of the Nazarene, the Board of General Superintendents' conclusion stated, "We believe that human nature, and ultimately *society*, can be radically and permanently changed by the grace of God."[6] This fundamental affirmation of grace undergirds all Wesleyan-Holiness beliefs and practices in the city.

---

3 Lovett H. Weems, Jr., *John Wesley's Message Today* (Nashville: Abingdon Press, 1991), 22–23.

4 Mildred Bangs Wynkoop, *A Theology of Love: The Dynamic of Wesleyanism* (Kansas City, MO: Beacon Hill Press of Kansas City, 1972), 100.

5 Timothy L. Smith, *Nazarenes and the Wesleyan Mission: Can We Learn from Our History?* (Kansas City, MO: Beacon Hill Press of Kansas City, 1979), 2. Originally, this was an address delivered at the Church of the Nazarene's annual leadership conference in January 1979. Smith's stated purpose for the address was "simply to ask what lessons learned from the long history of Methodism's relation to the doctrine of Christian holiness will help Nazarenes keep it in its central place in our faith and fellowship."

6 The Board of General Superintendents, "A Living Faith: What Nazarenes Believe—Core Values." Emphasis added.

The Quadrilateral

Many have suggested that John Wesley was not a systematic theologian in the same vein as the Continental Reformers who developed intricate doctrinal constructs.[7] Given his pragmatic bent as a man of action, some have wondered if Wesley had a systematic schema at all. The point is validated in that the closest document to a systematic theology written by Wesley, *A Plain Account of Christian Perfection*, reads more like a catechism than a systematic theology. There are good reasons for this. When we reflect on Wesley's background, we remember he was trained as an Anglican priest in the Church of England, and was a spiritual heir of the English Reformation.

At the behest of Henry VII, the archbishop of Canterbury and others traveled to Geneva to consider the advantages and disadvantages of a similar religious movement in the Magisterial Reformation.[8] Ultimately choosing a different approach than their ecumenical contemporaries, "the Church of England intentionally constructed a theological 'middle way,' a *via media* between Reformed Protestantism and Roman Catholicism."[9] Among other things, this middle way embraced the classical *solas* of the Protestant Reformation.[10] However, the Church of England's overarching concern was that the Reformed doctrine of *sola Scriptura* ("Scripture alone") was literalistic enough to be considered dangerously narrow. This perception caused the English Reformers to balance what they perceived as too limited a view of hermeneutics with other sources of doctrinal authority. "While accepting the primary authority of Scripture, the English divines felt strongly the other authorities, reason and tradition in particular, should

---

7 Kenneth L. Carder, "What Difference Does Knowing Wesley Make?" in *Rethinking Wesley's Theology for Contemporary Methodism*, ed. Randy L. Maddox (Nashville: Kingswood Books, 1998), 22. For the sake of reference and comparison, the final, 1559 edition of John Calvin's *Institutes of the Christian Religion* (Latin: Institutio Christianae Religionis) contained seventy-nine chapters. Based on the Apostles' Creed, Calvin focused the four divisions of his systematic theology on: "I believe in God the Father; I believe in Jesus Christ; I believe in the Holy Spirit; I believe in the holy catholic church."

8 The Magisterial Reformation (in contrast with the Radical Reformation) relates to those reform movements that were supported by ruling authorities (i.e., magistrates). Martin Luther, John Calvin, and Ulrich Zwingli were all backed in some measure by political powers to enforce their theological positions. "Magisterial" is also characterized by an emphasis on the authority of a teacher, often criticized by Radical Reformers as being similar to the power of Roman Catholic popes.

9 William M. Greathouse, "The Theological Vision That Guides Clergy Preparation in the Church of the Nazarene," *Didache: Faithful Teaching* Vol. 1, No. 1 (June 2001), http://didache.nazarene.org/index.php/volume-1-1/93-vini-greathouse/file.

10 The five classical *solas* of the Protestant Reformation include *sola Scriptura* ("by Scripture alone"), *sola fide* ("by faith alone"), *sola gratia* ("by grace alone"), *solo Christo* ("through Christ alone"), and *soli Deo gloria* ("glory to God alone").

also have a place in formulating theology." Accordingly, instead of constructing a formal systematic theology, the Church of England's efforts were focused on "practical divinity."[11] The Thirty-nine Articles of Religion replaced formal creeds, and *The Book of Common Prayer* became the liturgical guide for every Anglican parish.

This hallowed spiritual environment was the one in which John Wesley was nurtured. Born the son of an Anglican cleric and educated at Christ Church, Oxford, Wesley became a devout professor, pastor, and missionary of high-church Anglicanism and was a loyal churchman. However, through the influence of Peter Bohler and the Moravians, the devotional writings of William Law, Bishop Jeremy Taylor, and Thomas à Kempis, and his own cherished Aldersgate experience a week before his thirty-sixth birthday, Wesley was led to a new perspective on Christian experience. Like the Anglicans before him, his collection of sermons and written commentaries became the guiding teaching source and interpretive authority for Methodist preachers. He also affirmed Anglicanism's "threefold fount of guidance and authority"—that is, Scripture, reason, and tradition.[12] But Wesley's observations of others and his personal impressions led him to add another criterion for testing moral truth—the practical divinity of Christian experience. This addition in no way exalted the subjective whims, moods, attitudes, and opinions of individuals over Scripture or tradition. For Wesley, Christian experience was the recognition of "the centrality of the Person and work of the Holy Spirit in the life of the church," and the acknowledgment that the Spirit was the source of experience in the life of a believer.[13]

Concerning this important aspect of Wesley's viewpoint, Tom Noble writes: "This awareness of God's gracious 'presence' is what Wesley meant by 'experience,' and it was for him as real and unmistakable a perception as any sensory awareness might be. Spiritual experience comes when, to complement our five physical senses, the Holy Spirit gives us the spiritual sense to be aware of the presence of the reality of God. The inner subjective response is a response by the

---

11 William M. Greathouse, "What Are the Wesleyan Distinctives That Shape and Inform Christian Higher Education Today?" Presented at the inauguration of President Robert I. Brower, Point Loma Nazarene University, San Diego (April 16, 1998).

12 Don Thorsen, *The Wesleyan Quadrilateral: A Model of Evangelical Theology* (Lexington, KY: Emeth Press, 2005), 39.

13 Greathouse, "Wesleyan Distinctives," 2.

Spirit to the objective reality of the true and living God who encounters us."[14] William Greathouse suggests this connection between the Holy Spirit and experience was "the truly new and revolutionary aspect of John Wesley's theology."[15] Then, in a stirring synopsis, Greathouse expands the thought:

> It was John Wesley's understanding of the indispensable role of the Holy Spirit in the life of believers that gave to his theology a new focus, source, and form. In his recognition of the role of the Spirit in Christian experience, the Anglican Trilateral (Scripture, reason, and tradition) became "the Wesleyan Quadrilateral" (Scripture, tradition, reason, and experience). The new *focus* of Wesley's faith and ethic was on "holiness of heart and life," or Christian perfection; its new *source* was experience; its new *form*, "the restoration of the neglected doctrine of holiness to its merited position in the Protestant understanding of Christianity."[16]

The phrase "Wesleyan quadrilateral" was coined in 1964 by Albert Outler in his watershed study called simply *John Wesley*.[17] Wesley himself never used the phrase, nor did he suggest these terms as a methodological formula for ensuring proper orthodoxy, but throughout his writings and sermons these four elements are recurring themes that he held up as sources of authority for Christian theology.

However, for Wesley, Scripture was the primary authority. Weems states that "each of the four [Scripture, tradition, reason, experience] are interdependent and no one can be subsumed by the other. . . . All four guidelines should instruct all our theological reflection."[18] Conversely, Maddox suggests that "Wesley's so-called 'quadrilateral' of theological authorities could be more adequately described as a unilateral *rule* of Scripture within a trilateral *hermeneutic* of reason, tradition, and experience."[19] Others have written extensively regarding both the linguistic and

---

14 T. A. Noble, *Holy Trinity: Holy People: The Theology of Christian Perfecting* (Eugene, OR: Cascade Books, 2013), 16.

15 Greathouse, "Wesleyan Distinctives," 2.

16 Greathouse, "Wesleyan Distinctives," 2. Final quote from George Croft Cell, *The Rediscovery of John Wesley* (New York: Henry Holt and Company, 1935), 359.

17 Albert C. Outler, ed., *John Wesley* (New York: Oxford University Press, 1964).

18 Weems, *John Wesley's Message Today*, 12.

19 Maddox, *Responsible Grace*, 46. Maddox is elaborating on a phrase first coined by John Giffin in "Scriptural Standards in Religion: John Wesley's Letters to William Law and James Hervey," *Studia Biblica et Theologica* 16:143–68.

existential problems with a strict quadrilateral.[20] Regardless of the terminology used, however, these sources of authority continue to serve the Wesleyan-Holiness tradition as "the criteria by which theological ideas can be tested for truth," and they remain vital to any purposeful ecclesiology for the city.[21]

Means of Grace

Wesley talked often about the means of grace. He believed that while God's grace cannot be earned (it is free grace), Christians also do not idly stand by, waiting to receive grace. Instead, they actively engage in the means of grace— practices and habits that facilitate the administering of grace in the lives of Christians and those around them. The means of grace are not salvific themselves; rather, they are the various ways that God works to provide daily strength, abiding peace, renewing faith, spiritual power, and a pure heart to God's children. In summary, they are the mediums through which God's grace works to make us holy.

While Wesley never *intended* to be anything other than Anglican, he and his followers were given the name "Methodists" because "they prescribed certain methods or practices for growth in Christlikeness."[22] In a sermon with the same title, Wesley expressly defined the means of grace as "outward signs, words, or actions, ordained of God, and appointed for this end, to be the ordinary channels whereby he might convey to men, preventing, justifying, or sanctifying grace."[23] By devoting entire sermons to the means of grace, and insisting on their practice in Methodist communities of faith, Wesley emphasized their importance to healthy and balanced spiritual formation.

Wesleyan scholar Thorsen underscores this distinctive emphasis: "Unlike Calvin, Wesley thought that God preveniently used the means of grace to call people to salvation as well as for working in and through them. . . . In this regard,

---

20 For a comprehensive treatment of the current tensions within Wesleyan studies pertaining to Outler's quadrilateral, see Noble, *Holy Trinity*, 12–18.

21 Diane Leclerc, *Discovering Christian Holiness: The Heart of Wesleyan-Holiness Theology* (Kansas City, MO: Beacon Hill Press of Kansas City, 2010), 320. Leclerc christened the quadrilateral as simply a "name for Wesley's practice of checks and balances."

22 Ron Benefiel, "Our Wesleyan Tradition: Wesleyan Faith and Practice and the PLNU Mission," *Didache: Faithful Teaching*, Vol. 12, No. 2 (Winter 2013), http://didache.nazarene.org/index.php/volume-12-2/878-didache-v12n2-01-our-wesleyan-tradition-plnu/file.

23 John Wesley, *The Complete Works of John Wesley: Developments in Doctrine & Theological System, Volume 1, Sermons 1–53* (Harrington, DE: Delmarva Publications, 2014), Kindle Location 4000.

Wesley's emphasis on the prevenient nature of grace affirmed that God and people work—albeit mysteriously—together for their conversion, perseverance, and spiritual growth. God intends that the means of grace should include responsible action on the part of people."[24]

Wesley's belief that God's Spirit works continuously and cooperatively, even outside of the church, caused him to delineate between instituted and prudential means of grace. Instituted (appointed) were the means of grace established by God in the Scriptures; prudential (wise) were the means of grace not explicitly stated as such in the Bible but found to be beneficial in the pursuit of Christlikeness. Prudential practices for Wesley included but were not limited to "watching, denying ourselves, taking up our cross, and exercise of the presence of God."[25]

The means of grace can be divided into two categories: works of piety and works of mercy. Works of piety are primarily what we do to enhance our personal relationship with Christ. Works of mercy are what we do to engage God's ministry and mission in the world. Both have an individual component (what one can do alone) and a communal component (what must be done with the help of others). Individual works of piety include meditating on Scripture, faithfully attending worship, sharing faith with others (evangelism), praying, and fasting. Communal works of piety include participation in the sacraments, accountability (also known as Christian conferencing), Bible study, and preaching. The balance of both piety and mercy is needed to keep one from drifting to one extreme or the other. Piety without mercy becomes insular and compassionless; mercy without piety becomes mere political activism. Ministry in the city calls for both.

Christian Conferencing

Understanding the propensity of sin in the hearts of people and the tenacious temptation to live isolated lives, Wesley believed that every growing Christian needed accountable relationships and disciplined practices. While a new birth is necessary to begin new life in Christ, it is only the beginning. Christians are born; disciples are made. The Christian journey is initiated, encompassed, and empowered by God's grace, but a committed personal participation with God's

---

24 Thorsen, *Calvin vs. Wesley*, 55–56.

25 John Wesley, "Minutes of Several Conversations," in *The Works of the Rev. John Wesley, A.M.*, ed. Thomas Jackson (London: Wesleyan Methodist Book Room, 1872; reprinted Grand Rapids: Baker Book House, 1979), 8.323–24. Quoted in Thorsen, *Calvin vs. Wesley*, 56.

grace is both needed and expected. For Wesley, this participation was accomplished through a means of nurturing discipleship and church renewal that he referred to as Christian conferencing.

Different levels of Christian conferencing existed within Wesley's structure of discipleship. The first level was the Methodist society. A society was a geographically located group of fifty to a hundred people, comparable to a local parish. However, Wesley did not intend for these societies to replace regular worship services, and he was careful not to allow society meetings to interfere with the attendance of Anglican church services.[26] His loyalty to the Church of England continued despite the development of the societies. The first Methodist society was begun in 1739 in response to the needs Wesley sensed from a group of people who wanted to deepen their Christian walk. The fundamental purposes of the societies were "to pray together, to receive the word of exhortation, and to watch over one another in love, that they may help each other to work out their salvation."[27] In D. Michael Henderson's treatment of Wesley's system of discipleship groups, he points out, "The primary function of the society was cognitive instruction; it was the educational channel by which the tenets of Methodism were presented."[28]

The second level of conferencing was the class meeting. As a subdivision of the societies, the class meetings became early Methodism's most effective method of discipleship, and perhaps Wesley's greatest structural contribution to the life of holiness. If the society was the cognitive mode of discipleship, Henderson refers to the class meeting as "the behavioral mode," emphasizing the practical design and environment best suited for spiritual transformation.[29]

The third level of conferencing was the band, which facilitated what Henderson has termed "affective redirection." The bands were small groups of five to ten people, voluntary in nature, and intended for more intimate spiritual conversations between those with shared affinities—e.g., age, gender, marital status. The more intimate nature of the bands allowed for the probing accountability of examining motives, attitudes, blind spots, and emotions. Henderson maintains that the band was Wesley's personal favorite. It was philosophically closest to his

---

26 D. Michael Henderson, *John Wesley's Class Meeting: A Model for Making Disciples* (Nappanee, IN: Francis Asbury Press of Evangel Publishing House, 1997), 85.

27 Wesley, *Works* (Jackson), 8:269.

28 Henderson, *John Wesley's Class Meeting*, 84.

29 Henderson, *John Wesley's Class Meeting*, 93.

experience at the Holy Club in Oxford and, later, the experiment of close conversations from the Fetter Lane Society in London.[30]

Other levels of conferencing included the select societies and penitent bands. The select society was the "training mode," reserved for an exclusive group of men and women considered to be present and future leaders of the movement.[31] The mentoring culture of the select societies was crucial to providing a regular stream of capably trained leaders for every level of Methodism. Wesley viewed them as a think tank to strategize future developments within the movement. Unlike any other conferencing group, the select societies had no formal leader or set agenda other than to allow for peer learning and honest conversations. Wesley continued active participation in a select society until at least two years before his death.[32]

Penitent bands functioned as the "rehabilitative mode," designed for those who were struggling with grave personal issues of addictions or other deep-seated areas of moral or social dysfunction in their lives.[33] Alcoholism, for example, was a societal scourge in eighteenth-century England and destroyed families in epidemic proportions.[34] The groups met often during times when the penitents would be most tempted to revisit their former lifestyles, and they held the participants to a strict format of accountability and use of time. Several modern recovery systems, such as Alcoholics Anonymous and Celebrate Recovery, have benefited from Wesley's penitent band model.

While all levels of Christian conferencing were a vital means of grace for Wesley's Methodists, the class meeting was the engine that drove the movement. Through trial and error with various forms of groups, Wesley came to believe that the class meeting was the heart of Christian community and vital to growing in Christlikeness. It became the method of Methodism. Once it was thoroughly tested through experience and confirmed as effective for producing fruitful disciples, Wesley implored his followers, "Never omit meeting your class

---

30 Henderson, *John Wesley's Class Meeting*, 112–13.

31 Henderson, *John Wesley's Class Meeting*, 121. Often, these select men and women were personally selected by John Wesley.

32 Robert G. Tuttle, Jr., *John Wesley: His Life and Theology* (Grand Rapids: Zondervan, 1978), 27. Tuttle notes that on June 28, 1799, Wesley's eighty-fifth birthday, he journaled about his attendance at a select society.

33 Henderson, *John Wesley's Class Meeting*, 125.

34 Henderson, *John Wesley's Class Meeting*, 19. "One of the most demoralizing vices of the poor was widespread alcoholism, even among the children. In 1736, every sixth house in London was licensed as a grogshop. Gin consumption topped eleven million gallons a year in England alone."

or band. . . . These are the very sinews of our society. And whatever weakens or tends to weaken our regard for these, or our exactness in attending them, strikes at the very root of our community."[35]

Wesley's discipleship methods were highly structured and systematically designed. Each Methodist society was divided into smaller groups of up to twelve people. Each class met weekly, with a designated leader who was responsible for giving direction to the class meetings and ensuring the pastoral care of each of its members, especially new believers. Each society member was required to attend a class meeting. Failure to do so over a period of time meant expulsion from the society. One paragraph from Wesley's Rules of the United Societies, written in 1744, outlines the agenda for every class meeting and the job description of each leader:

> That it may the more easily be discerned whether they are indeed working out their own salvation, each society is divided into smaller companies called "classes," according to their respective places of abode. There are about twelve persons in every class, one of whom is styled the Leader. It is his business: (1) To see each person in his class once a week at least, in order to inquire how their souls prosper; to advise, reprove, comfort, or exhort, as occasion may require; to receive what they are willing to give toward the relief of the poor; (2) To meet the minister and the stewards of the society once a week; to pay to the stewards what they have received of their several classes in the week preceding; and to show their account of what each person has contributed.[36]

There are several points to clarify here.

First, each class was established based on where a person lived and not on personal interests, age, gender, social standing, or level of spiritual maturity. They were small neighborhood groups from mixed backgrounds and capacities.

---

35 John Wesley, *A Plain Account of Christian Perfection, Annotated*, Randy L. Maddox and Paul W. Chilcote, eds. (Kansas City, MO: Beacon Hill Press of Kansas City, 2015), 142–43. Wesley's *Plain Account* underwent several revisions during his lifetime, the last edit recognized by most scholars to have been in 1777.

36 John Wesley, "The Nature, Design, and General Rules of the United Societies," in *The Works of John Wesley, Bicentennial Edition* (Nashville: Abingdon Press, 1989), 9:69–70.

Second, while Wesley used the masculine pronoun to describe the group leader, women often served as leaders of class meetings, including a number of women preachers, an atypical arrangement for the time.[37]

Third, people were in class to ask questions regarding the spiritual progress of each member. They were not there for Bible studies or Christian education; those things were reserved for the societies. They were there to ask the question, "How goes it with your soul?" or, as historians have recently rephrased the question, "How is your life with God?"[38]

Fourth, there was an expectation that each person would give what they could to support the poor.[39] The members were not allowed to become insulated from the social ills outside their walls. Rather, they were called to the ethical and compassionate response that holiness of heart and life demanded.[40] In so doing, they also fulfilled the general rules of a Methodist: "to do no harm; to do good to both the bodies and souls of their neighbors; and attend upon the ordinances of God."[41] The class leader would then follow up with society leadership to give a full report of what had happened in the meeting, communicate the spiritual needs of the members, and deliver the funds collected for the poor.

The class meeting was so central to Methodist life that attendance continued to be a formal requirement in the Methodist Episcopal Church for several decades. For a period of time, Methodists issued class-meeting tickets to people quarterly. They could use the tickets to gain admittance into the larger worship services.[42] Though the class meeting had a significant impact on the Methodists in Great Britain, its greatest results manifested in American Methodism. In 1776, Congregationalists, Episcopalians, and Presbyterians dominated the religious scene of colonial America, with a combined 55 percent of all religious adherents. Methodists, a very small sect in 1776, accounted for a minuscule 2.5 percent of colonial church life, with a meager sixty-five churches. By 1850—just seven decades later—the Method-

---

37 Henry H. Knight III and F. Douglas Powe, Jr., *Transforming Community: The Wesleyan Way to Missional Congregations* (Nashville: Discipleship Resources, 2016), Kindle Location 363.

38 Elaine A. Heath and Scott T. Kisker, *Longing for Spring: A New Vision for Wesleyan Community* (Eugene, OR: Cascade Books, 2010), 34. Quoted in Kevin M. Watson, *The Class Meeting: Reclaiming a Forgotten (and Essential) Small Group Experience* (Franklin, TN: Seedbed Publishing, 2014), 25.

39 David Hempton, *Methodism: Empire of the Spirit* (New Haven, CT: Yale University Press, 2005), Kindle Locations 1041–48.

40 It should be noted that the first official experiment with a class meeting was a capital campaign to help pay off a building debt in Bristol.

41 Knight and Powe, *Transforming Community*, Kindle Locations 387–400.

42 Watson, *The Class Meeting*, 28, 29.

ists were the largest denomination in the United States with 13,302 congregations, representing more than one-third of all American church members.[43]

Many factors contributed to what Roger Finke and Rodney Stark have called "the meteoric rise of Methodism."[44] Two of the most important factors include the missionary spirit of Methodists to break down socioeconomic and racial barriers,[45] and the prominent place of the doctrine of entire sanctification in the preaching, teaching, and experience of the people.[46]

Nevertheless, scholars agree that, underneath these factors for the Methodists' surprising success in colonial, and later frontier, America is the implicit impact of the class meetings on the American Methodist laity. Kevin Watson maintains, "[Because] every Methodist throughout this period was expected to participate in a weekly class meeting, a strong case can be made that the class meeting was the single most important factor of early Methodism and to the retention of converts within Methodism. People who had come to faith in Christ were immediately placed in a class meeting, where they would be helped to grow in their faith and where they could learn how to practice their faith."[47] Watson continues, saying that Wesley felt that "if the class meeting was threatened, then the 'very root' (Wesley's phrase) was in danger."[48]

---

43 Roger Finke and Rodney Stark, *The Churching of America, 1776–2005: Winners and Losers in Our Religious Economy* (New Brunswick, NJ: Rutgers University Press, 2005), 55–57.

44 Finke and Stark, *The Churching of America*, 55–57.

45 Led by the uncompromising John Wesley, the majority of British and American Methodists were vehemently opposed to slavery and were active in the struggle against it. It is widely believed that John Wesley's final letter was written to William Wilberforce to encourage him in the antislavery fight in England. As a result, Methodists and Baptists were the most welcoming to black Americans. Black Methodist pastors were supported, and black Methodist laypersons were encouraged into leadership roles. The support given to the African-American community caused an explosion of growth in Methodism. By 1851 the Methodist Episcopal Church enjoyed a membership of 7.8 percent of all black adults in the United States (Finke and Stark, *The Churching of America*, 101). One of the most powerful witnesses to this racial acceptance came from Richard Allen, a free African-American Methodist preacher from Philadelphia. He believed that Methodism, as opposed to other American denominations, "provided the personal discipline and reform needed for people being held in bondage" (Finke and Stark, *The Churching of America*, 104). Nash states, "To Allen and other black Methodist leaders it seemed a perfect system for lifting up an oppressed people" (Gary B. Nash, *Forging Freedom: The Formation of Philadelphia's Black Community, 1720–1840* [Cambridge: Harvard University Press, 1988], 193. Quoted in Finke and Stark, *The Churching of America*, 104).

46 C. C. Goss, *Statistical History of the First Century of American Methodism: A Summary of the Origin and Present Operations of Other Denominations* (New York: Carlton & Porter, 1866), 162–86. Quoted in Finke and Stark, *The Churching of America*, 113–16. Goss outlined in great detail the reasons for the success of the "Methodist Miracle," on the occasion of the celebration of one hundred years of Methodism.

47 Watson, *The Class Meeting*, 22.

48 Watson, *The Class Meeting*, 27.

The concern was warranted, and proved to be true. While no specific time can be pinpointed, historians agree that the Methodist class meeting in the United States began its decline in the mid-nineteenth century.[49] Timothy Smith observes: "The urgent appeals of leaders in the American Holiness Movement for their revival indicates that in many *urban congregations* class meetings were either moribund or extinct."[50]

Contributing factors to the decline of the class meeting have been postulated, including upward mobility among Methodism's members, busier lives in urban settings, and the rise of Sunday school.[51] The popularity of Sunday school is a legitimate argument for the atrophy of the class meeting. The Sunday school movement, for all the good it provided, began to replace the accountability of the class meeting with information-based Christian education led by a teacher. Phoebe Palmer added a popular new institution to urban Methodism called the Tuesday Meeting for the Promotion of Holiness. It began in New York City in 1836, but by mid-century, it had spread to hundreds of towns and cities across the country, and the prayer meeting began to supersede the class meeting. There were also ministers' weekly prayer meetings in cities and the increasing expansion of the camp meeting to be attended.[52] In short, with the swelling menu of options that came with the American Holiness Movement, the class meeting became optional. It is not a coincidence that, as American Methodism "began to distance itself from the class meeting, its growth also began to decrease, then stop, and finally decline."[53]

What happened in people's lives in the atmosphere of a class meeting was significant. To remove a primary means of grace—by which Wesleyan-Holiness Christians cultivated their pursuit of holiness—without replacing it was not without consequence. The genius of Wesley's small group organization of authenticity, accountability, support, and care remains a missing piece in many congregations today. People thrive in high-trust networks of holy love. The class meeting's purpose is vital to sustaining urban congregations in the Wesleyan-Holiness tradition.

---

49 Smith, "Nazarenes and the Wesleyan Mission," 7–10.

50 Smith, "Nazarenes and the Wesleyan Mission," 8. Emphasis added.

51 Smith, "Nazarenes and the Wesleyan Mission," 8–10.

52 Smith, "Nazarenes and the Wesleyan Mission," 8.

53 Watson, *The Class Meeting*, 31, 151. "A variety of other explanations can also be seen to account for the numerical decline of Methodism over the last several decades. I am not making a formal academic argument here. Nevertheless, the decline of the class meeting is frequently included by historians of Methodism as at least *a* factor in the broader decline of American Methodism, if not the most important factor." Emphasis added.

Works of Mercy and the Poor

Wesley's emphasis on ministry to the poor is well documented. The class meetings received regular offerings for the poor as an act of compassion and a practice of Christian stewardship. However, it is important to stress that Wesley believed working with and among the poor is not merely an act of compassion but is also a necessary aspect of the spiritual formation of every Christian. Thus, he maintained that living with the poor is a work of mercy and a work of piety.

Wesley believed the gospel was good news to the poor. He made a practice of "visiting the poor as a *spiritual discipline*, and encouraged—indeed, insisted—that his Methodists do the same."[54] Even as an elderly man, Wesley risked his own health and well-being in the cold of winter, trudging through ankle-deep snow to go publicly begging for funds on behalf of the suffering.[55] Theodore Jennings elaborates, "Every aspect of Methodism was subjected to the criterion, how will this benefit the poor?"[56] However, it was more than concern for the comfort of the poor that motivated Wesley; it was vitally important to him because he saw no other way to understand or identify with the poor than to be among them.[57] For that reason, Wesley believed it was far better "to *carry* relief to the poor, than to *send* it" because of the spiritual impact it would have on the one bringing the help.[58] Jennings further asserts that this regular practice of visitation was not mere sympathy or sentimentalism but that, for Wesley, "visiting the poor and sick and imprisoned was a *means of grace*, to be ranked alongside private and public prayer or the sacraments themselves."[59]

Randy Maddox points out that many contemporary writers on Wesleyan spirituality view works of mercy "mainly as ways in which we *express* our spirituality and not ways in which we *develop* it."[60] Thus, Wesley's understanding of ministry to and with the marginalized poor, sick, and imprisoned was more than mere

---

54 Lovett H. Weems, Jr., *Leadership in the Wesleyan Spirit* (Nashville: Abingdon Press, 1999), 47. Emphasis added.

55 Weems, *Leadership in the Wesleyan Spirit*, 47.

56 Theodore W. Jennings, Jr., "Wesley's Preferential Option for the Poor," *Quarterly Review* 9 (1989), 16.

57 Theodore W. Jennings, Jr., *Good News to the Poor: John Wesley's Evangelical Economics* (Nashville: Abingdon Press, 1990), 54.

58 John Wesley, *Journal* (November 24, 1760), in *Works* (Jackson), 3:28.

59 Jennings, *Good News to the Poor*, 54. Emphasis added.

60 Randy L. Maddox, "'Visit the Poor': John Wesley, the Poor, and the Sanctification of Believers" in *The Poor and the People Called Methodists, 1729–1999*, ed. Richard P. Heitzenrater (Nashville: Kingswood Books, 2002), 64. Emphasis added.

compassion; as a means of grace for the Christian, this kind of ministry is indispensable to Wesleyan spirituality. These acts of mercy become the ways by which God works to establish the character of holiness in God's people and to give growth in grace toward the recovery of the divine image. Benefiel summarizes, "For us to grow in Christlikeness, as God intended, we must engage in activities through which God's mercy is conveyed to others."[61]

Emphasis on the poor as a means of grace began to wane as Methodism matured after Wesley's death. Nathan Hatch observes that by the 1840s American Methodists were not only the largest Protestant denomination in the country, but—like their Presbyterian and Congregationalist counterparts—had begun their own journey toward the "inevitable allure of respectability."[62] They were no longer the newcomer, marginalized sect on American soil; Methodists had become successful businessmen, bankers, politicians, and educators. Methodist church buildings began to change to accommodate the new affluence. Pipe organs and stained-glass windows were installed in Methodist sanctuaries. Soon followed the practice of pew rentals, which were a way to raise congregational funds to pay for elaborate facilities, but they also further segregated the more prestigious Methodist members from other church members. Even the teaching of the doctrine of entire sanctification began to diminish to make room for more progressive ethical concerns.

Wesley was well aware of the danger of riches. He recognized that the life of holiness would lead to an increased social standing and economic prosperity. When people become industrious, disciplined, responsible, and honest, they will be set apart from the masses, particularly in an industrialized society, and material success will soon follow.[63] Sociologists have characterized this phenomenon as redemption and lift.[64] While Wesley predicted the vulnerability, and although he preached a number of sermons on the corrupting power of riches, he was less concerned that Methodists would become wealthy and more concerned that in their newly found societal elevation they would neglect their calling to the poor.[65]

---

61 Benefiel, "Our Wesleyan Tradition," 13.

62 Nathan O. Hatch, *The Democratization of American Christianity* (New Haven, CT: Yale University Press, 1989), 127.

63 Jennings, *Good News to the Poor*, 135.

64 Donald A. McGavran, *Understanding Church Growth* (Grand Rapids: Wm. B. Eerdmans Publishing Co., 1970), 295.

65 Richard M. Cameron, *Methodism and Society in Historical Perspective* (Nashville: Abingdon Press, 1961), 73.

His fears proved true. Slowly, the rising refinement of the Methodists began to alienate them from the people early Methodism had been so careful to include.

The changing atmosphere did not go unnoticed. Prominent Methodists began to speak out against the injustice. In an effort not to lose this vital connection with the poor, outspoken leaders like B. T. Roberts (of the Free Methodists), William Booth (of the Salvation Army), and, later, Phineas Bresee began to call for a recapturing of the original vision for the poor. Bresee left a distinguished ecclesiastical career to return to his passion of ministry to and with the poor. Nazarene church buildings and formal dress were intentionally made less pretentious and more simplified so the poor would feel welcome and comfortable. Bresee's passion for the poor was so keenly felt that he wrote to the first Nazarenes, "The evidence of the presence of Jesus in our midst is that we bear the gospel, particularly to the poor."[66] While Bresee's care for the poor may have been partially influenced by the postmillennialist eschatology of his day, he recognized it as a necessary aspect of true religion and faithful discipleship.

Donald Dayton contends that, while Wesley's move toward the poor was central to his Christian praxis, he did not ground it in a confessional theological dogma. According to Dayton, Wesley's followers in the American Holiness Movement "more clearly articulated a theological grounding for the Wesleyan option for the poor and *made it constitutive of the Gospel.*"[67] For the American Holiness leaders, "one cannot know and serve Jesus Christ without friendship with the poor."[68]

Compassionate acts that serve the poor and oppressed are an important part of engaging in Christ's incarnational ministry and advancing the kingdom of God. Additionally, what God will accomplish in these interactions is also a means of grace for every believer. Discipleship in Wesleyan-Holiness ecclesiology depends on the pursuit of Christlikeness *and* ministry to and with the marginalized. These practices of the Christian life "are not simply duties, they are also gracious means that God has provided to free us to become progressively the kind of people that we really long to be."[69]

---

66 P. F. Bresee, *Nazarene Messenger*, December 31, 1901.

67 Donald Dayton, "Liberation Theology in the Wesleyan and Holiness Tradition," *Online Journal of Public Theology*. Emphasis in original.

68 Carder, "What Difference Does Knowing Wesley Make?" 29.

69 Maddox, "Visit the Poor," 81.

A Church for the City
Kirche in Aktion (Germany)

What would it look like to see heaven on earth? This is the question that has fueled the work of *Kirche in Aktion* (English: Church in Action), a network of urban churches in Germany's Rhine-Main region. Rev. Dr. Philip Zimmermann began the first KIA congregation in the city of Mainz, Germany, in 2008, and his brother, Rev. Cris Zimmermann, joined soon after. There are now KIA congregations—or what they call kingdom communities—in the nearby cities of Frankfurt, Offenbach, Darmstadt, and Wiesbaden.

As third-generation ministers, Pastors Philip and Cris are passionate about seeing heaven come to earth in their cities, yet they are also aware of the church's limitations in post-Christian German culture. It required so much effort to get someone into a church building, they began to wonder: what would it look like if, instead of asking people to come to the church, the church went to where the people are? Each kingdom community began and continues regular worship in a public setting such as a restaurant, coffee shop, bar, theater, or retirement home.

But Pastor Philip will tell you that the most important element of the KIA churches are the Communities on Mission. These are groups of eight to twelve people who meet once a week, alternating between a Bible study one week and serving together the next. Each KIA kingdom community congregation is made up of multiple Communities on Mission, with each one dedicated to a specific area in which they serve and develop relationships. Whether they spend time in brothels, refugee camps, rest homes, or homeless encampments, the focus is more on presence and solidarity than on fixing.

Perhaps the best part of these groups is that they are open to whoever wants to join them, and are often the first entry point for newcomers. Those who are searching for a meaningful life are eager to join a cause that addresses social needs in their community. They receive an invitation not only into the work but also into a community of relationships, conversations, and belief. There are now countless stories of individuals being transformed by Jesus as they seek to participate in the transformation of their city.

In fact, these groups are so foundational and transformational that the pastors of KIA have committed themselves to starting and supporting one thousand Communities on Mission in the church's second decade so that ten thousand people can be engaged in heaven on earth each week. They have also begun partnerships and training opportunities for urban churches outside of Germany—particularly in the United States.

"My hope," says Pastor Philip, "is that every Christian would be able to know the answer to these two questions: Whom am I sent *to*? And whom am I sent *with*?" This, he says, is what distinguishes the church of Jesus Christ from social enterprise or political agenda: we are people joining God's mission, together.

For Reflection or Discussion

1. Of the Wesleyan-Holiness distinctives discussed in this chapter, which one(s) have you seen emphasized in your own church experience? Are there any that have not been present?

2. Can you imagine a structure for John Wesley's system of groups for teaching, practices, and accountability for today? He also had groups for leadership development and active recovery. What would those kinds of groups look like in your context?

3. John Wesley firmly believed and taught that grace was powerful enough to transform individuals, as long as individuals actively engaged in and participated with the means of grace. How have you seen this to be true in your own life or in the lives of others?

City Practice
Spend Time among the Poor

It is hard to make decisions based on benefiting the poor—as Wesley urged his Methodists to do—if we do not know anyone who lives in poverty. This week, go out of your way to spend time among those who know what it means to be poor. Consider visiting a homeless shelter, a day center for adults with disability, the courthouse or county jail, or a recovery ministry. If you know someone connected to one of these communities, ask that person for permission to shadow them as they make their regular visits. While there, remember that your task is not to fix but to learn. What does good news look like for these neighbors? How might they experience freedom? Consider whether or how you can make this practice a regular part of your routine.

5

SCRIPTURAL FOUNDATIONS

Much has been written in recent biblical studies regarding the importance of literary genres and their rhetorical function. "Genre" refers to the form of the literature; "rhetorical function" refers to how the genre is intended to be used literarily, or "what a particular genre is designed to do in the reading process."[1] For example, in the literary genre of letters, a letter of resignation has a different purpose (rhetorical function) than a letter of recommendation. There are different forms of letters with various rhetorical functions, including forms *within* the form. A newspaper is a form of literature that has distinct, separate rhetorical purposes within its pages. There are headlines and editorials, obituaries and box scores, crosswords and weather reports. While they are all in the form (genre) of newspaper, these forms within the form have different functions, and each one must be read in light of its specific purpose.

Reading the literary genres of Scripture with an eye toward form and function helps ensure exegetical accuracy. The Nazarene Articles of Faith affirm that the sixty-six books of the Christian Scriptures are "given by divine inspiration, inerrantly revealing the will of God concerning us in all things necessary to our salvation."[2] However, the forms that Scripture takes to express the purpose of

---

1 Thomas G. Long, *Preaching and the Literary Forms of the Bible* (Philadelphia: Fortress Press, 1989), 24–25.

2 *Church of the Nazarene Manual: 2017–2021* (Kansas City, MO: Nazarene Publishing House, 2017), 27.

revealing the will of God are rich and varied. There are narratives and poems, historical records and genealogies, law and wisdom, songs and letters, prophets and gospels. And there are also forms within the forms. Take the book of Psalms, for example: there are psalms of thanksgiving, of lament, of ascent, and royal psalms. All of them comprise the Psalter, but there are different rhetorical functions intended to elicit different responses from the hearer or reader. To read a lament psalm with the same literary lens as a thanksgiving psalm would miss the power of the inspired Word's intent. Just as words matter, so also do forms.

This chapter will consider the particular form and function of a text from the Hebrew Scripture. While it is not a passage dealing specifically with urban life *per se*, it does offer the framework of what God intends life in community to be, and, as such, operates as a vision for churches in the city.

Isaiah 11: A Paradigm for Churches in Urban Contexts[3]

A shoot will come up from the stump of Jesse;
from his roots a Branch will bear fruit.
The Spirit of the LORD will rest on him—
the Spirit of wisdom and of understanding,
the Spirit of counsel and of might,
the Spirit of the knowledge and fear of the LORD—
and he will delight in the fear of the LORD.

He will not judge by what he sees with his eyes,
or decide by what he hears with his ears;
but with righteousness he will judge the needy,
with justice he will give decisions for the poor of the earth.
He will strike the earth with the rod of his mouth;
with the breath of his lips he will slay the wicked.
Righteousness will be his belt
and faithfulness the sash around his waist.

---

3 I first presented the content of this section in the keynote address at the John A. Knight Bible and Theology Conference, Mount Vernon Nazarene University, February 2012. The title of the address was "Lions, Lambs, and the New Creation: An Exploration of the Eschatological Vision of Isaiah 11 for the Church."

The wolf will live with the lamb,
the leopard will lie down with the goat,
the calf and the lion and the yearling together;
and a little child will lead them.
The cow will feed with the bear,
their young will lie down together,
and the lion will eat straw like the ox.
The infant will play near the cobra's den,
and the young child will put its hand into the viper's nest.
They will neither harm nor destroy
on all my holy mountain,
for the earth will be filled with the knowledge of the LORD
as the waters cover the sea.

In that day the Root of Jesse will stand as a banner for the peoples;
the nations will rally to him, and his resting place will be glorious.

(Isaiah 11:1–10)

The literary form of Isaiah 11 contains both prophetic and apocalyptic elements. Prophetic literature is more than foretelling or prediction; it is *forth*-telling and declarative. This knowledge is vitally important for understanding that apocalyptic literature is far more than mere end-time projections. James K. A. Smith notes that the point of apocalyptic literature is to "unveil the realities around us for what they really are."[4] Likewise, Eugene Peterson suggests that "the task of apocalyptic imagination is to provide images that show us what is going on in our lives" with the power "to wake us up" to what is perhaps hidden but most real.[5]

With these purposes in mind, the twofold rhetorical function of the prophetic and apocalyptic genres is to offer hope for the future and to serve as a paradigm for living today. It does not deny the reality of the way things are, but it looks with hope toward the way things will be. Biblical theologians have de-

---

4 James K. A. Smith, *Desiring the Kingdom: Worship, Worldview, and Cultural Formation*, Vol. 1 of *Cultural Liturgies* (Grand Rapids: Baker Academic, 2009), 92.

5 Eugene H. Peterson, *Reversed Thunder: The Revelation of John and the Praying Imagination* (San Francisco: HarperSanFrancisco, 1991), xii, 145–46.

scribed this apocalyptic viewpoint as the already and not-yet kingdom of God.[6] It is a call to a particular way for God's people to order their lives today, according to the way God will cause all things to be one day. Jesus taught his disciples to pray, "Your kingdom come, your will be done, on earth as it is in heaven" (Matthew 6:10). To paraphrase, the life of the Christian community now is a foretaste of heaven on earth.

The Greek word *eschaton* means "last things" or "end times" or "the climax of history."[7] A Christian, therefore, is someone who lives today based on what they know will be true tomorrow. This is a distinctive Wesleyan-Holiness view of living eschatologically. The apostle Paul alludes to this type of attitude in the beginning of his epistle to the Ephesians (1:13–14). As God's children, we have been given a rich inheritance in light of which we can live today. The basis of this hope is not just a future projection but the *arrabon*—the down payment—a foretaste of heaven that can be experienced now. "Thus, the Spirit-endowed church stands within the present age as a sign of what is to come, already prefiguring the redemption for which it waits."[8]

Reflecting on this concept, Alan Hirsch proposes that spiritual leadership in the already and not-yet kingdom means that we must learn to "manage from the future."[9] Hirsch goes on, "This means placing ourselves in the new future and then taking a series of steps, not in order to get there someday, but as if you are there, or almost there, now. . . . We are called to act in the knowledge that is already here *now* and yet will be completed *then*."[10]

With these foundational aspects of the literary function of Isaiah 11 defined, there are several key communal elements of the prophetic vision that inform a Wesleyan-Holiness approach to ministry in the urban context. The prophetic vision of Isaiah is a portrayal of God's perfect intention for life in the Christian

---

6   The phrase "already/not yet" that is so widespread today is first attributed to Reformed theologian and prominent Princeton Theological Seminary professor Geerhardus Vos, who taught biblical theology there from 1892 until his retirement in 1932.

7   Fleming Rutledge, *The Crucifixion: Understanding the Death of Jesus Christ* (Grand Rapids: Wm. B. Eerdmans Publishing Co., 2015), 220.

8   Richard B. Hays, *The Moral Vision of the New Testament: A Contemporary Introduction to New Testament Ethics* (San Francisco: HarperSanFrancisco, 1996), 21.

9   Hirsch gets the idea of managing from the future from Richard T. Pascale, Mark Millemann, and Linda Gioja, *Surfing the Edge of Chaos: The Laws of Nature and the New Laws of Business* (New York: Three Rivers Press, 2000), 240. Quoted in Alan Hirsch, *The Forgotten Ways: Reactivating the Missional Church* (Grand Rapids: Brazos Press, 2006), 234.

10   Hirsch, *The Forgotten Ways*, 234.

community, an ecclesiological description of what the church is called to be like today. The symbolic nature of apocalyptic language means that the language employed is poetry, not prose. This does not mean that the symbols are not reality. Apocalyptic symbolism "points to actual, though transcendent, reality, so the language can be called 'literal non-literalism.'"[11] Further, apocalyptic language utilizes "animals, colors, numbers, and other everyday entities" to "take on symbolic value . . . to express the nearly inexpressible."[12]

Isaiah 11 is a prototype of what the church is called to be and do. The animals named (leopards, goats, oxen, lions, and lambs) can be viewed as metaphors for the people of God. The messianic vision is a vivid depiction of what God's perfected new creation will look like when the entire world comes under the lordship of Jesus Christ—the fruitful Branch from the stump of Jesse. This prophetic passage has the rhetorical function of offering hope because it tells us what will be in God's new creation. It also functions rhetorically as a paradigm because it is an invitation for us to order our lives today in Christian community according to the way things will one day be for the whole world.

Isaiah's vision of a "peaceable kingdom"[13] is a compelling snapshot of what God's *shalom,* peace, completeness, fullness, and wholeness look like when God's kingdom begins to break in. It is important to note that *shalom* is not merely a personal state of well-being; *shalom* is a corporate concept: "It describes a community, not simply the interior well-being of an individual or a small group of people. *Shalom* captures the well-being of an entire society."[14] This is reflected in God's call through Jeremiah to work for the *shalom* of the city of Babylon (Jeremiah 29:7). *Shalom* cannot be privatized; it is thoroughly public.

Some contend that Isaiah's vision is only a description of what heaven will be like because this is not the way of the world today. Wolves do not live with

---

11 Attributed to John J. Collins (without reference) in Robert W. Wall, *New International Biblical Commentary: Revelation* (Peabody, MA: 1991), 15. Quoted in Michael J. Gorman, *Reading Revelation Responsibly: Uncivil Worship and Witness: Following the Lamb into the New Creation* (Eugene, OR: Cascade Books, 2011), 20.

12 Gorman, *Reading Revelation Responsibly,* 17.

13 Quaker minister and artist Edward Hicks coined this phrase for his first rendition of a painting on Isaiah 11 in 1834. He eventually produced sixty-one re-creations of the first painting.

14 Robert Linthicum, *Transforming Power: Biblical Strategies for Making a Difference in Your Community* (Downers Grove, IL: InterVarsity Press, 2003), 37. *Shalom* theology is also enriched by the writings of Walter Brueggemann, *Living Toward a Vision: Biblical Reflections on Shalom* (1982); Lisa Sharon Harper, *The Very Good Gospel: How Everything Wrong Can Be Made Right* (2016); and Randy Woodley, *Shalom and the Community of Creation: An Indigenous Vision* (2012).

lambs; leopards do not lie down with goats; calves and lions and yearlings do not coexist together. Indeed, lambs get eaten as wolves get fatter. However, if this scriptural vision is intended to be a paradigm for the way we are to construct our lives as the church today, it serves as a beautiful portrait of how God desires life to be shared among and through his people.

Though not exclusively urban in nature, the decision of Jesus to align his ministry with the Jubilee statements of Isaiah 61 indicates his commitment to bringing the kingdom of God to earth. This kingdom, which is the *shalom* community in action, will "bring in its wake a grand reversal in which poverty and systems of domination will be eliminated and humanity will become all that God intended it to be."[15] The church is a sign and symbol that God's kingdom is breaking into the world (known as "inaugurated eschatology").[16] In this way, the church becomes both word and witness to an unbelieving world. If the church is to move toward Isaiah's vision, there are at least four ecclesial values that must exist for this communal dream to become a reality in the city.

Inclusive Diversity

With Isaiah 11 as a framework, the first ecclesial value of Wesleyan-Holiness urban communities is inclusive diversity—or, dissimilar people coming together in spite of their differences. The opposite of inclusive diversity is exclusive selectivity. When a place is exclusive, such as country clubs and gated residential communities, it means that only particular kinds of people are welcome. Exclusive places are restricted by design, and many, if not most, require people to have similar socioeconomic backgrounds and interests. People join clubs and live in gated communities because they want to choose what kinds of friends and neighbors they will have.

An understanding of the church based on Isaiah 11 is the polar opposite of exclusive selectivity. No animal in the vision is asked to become like its opposite. The social environment of Isaiah 11 offers a warm embrace to every person and does not insist that everyone be, think, or act alike. Some proponents of the church-growth movement suggest that, for churches to grow, congregations

---

15 Linthicum, *Transforming Power*, 66.

16 George Eldon Ladd served as a pioneer of the study of inaugurated eschatology. First published in 1974, his classic work, *A Theology of the New Testament*, became a leading voice in the rise of kingdom theology.

must form themselves around homogeneous units. In *Understanding Church Growth*, Donald McGavran defines a homogeneous unit as "a section of society in which all the members have some characteristic in common."[17]

While McGavran's assessment may be sociologically simpler, it is not a biblical picture of Christian community. As people come to faith in Christ and are discipled toward Christlikeness, they must be integrated into the life of a diverse body of Christ that will not be homogeneous. To forget this basic kingdom principle can quickly lead to myopic tribalism and racial segregation. Soong-Chan Rah explains:

> The homogeneous unit principle yields a segregation that furthers racial conflict and alienation. Blindly adhering to the homogeneous unit principle, therefore, has resulted in an American evangelicalism incapable of dealing with the reality of a growing cultural pluralism and ethnic heterogeneity. *De facto*, segregation perpetuated by the church growth movement yielded a disenfranchisement of nonwhites from the larger evangelical movement as Western, white values of success shaped American evangelicalism's perception of success. The church growth movement served the function of furthering the defining of American evangelicalism by Western, white culture.[18]

If churches are to be effective, especially in the urban context, the homogeneous unit principle must be rejected. Soong-Chan Rah's research indicates that less than 4 percent of Christian congregations are racially integrated.[19] There is still much work to be done, but Isaiah's vision is clear: communities that reflect the kingdom of God cherish inclusivity. Dallas Willard plainly sets forth, "God's aim in human history is the creation of an inclusive community of loving persons, with himself included as its primary sustainer and most glorious inhabitant."[20]

Isaiah 11 does not promote homogeneity. Leopards, goats, oxen, bears, cobras, and children all coexist peacefully (vv. 6–9). This snapshot of the kingdom of God breaks down all potential barriers to Christian community—including gender,

---

17 Donald A. McGavran, *Understanding Church Growth* (Grand Rapids: Wm. B. Eerdmans Publishing Co., 1970), 69.

18 Soong-Chan Rah, *The Next Evangelicalism: Freeing the Church from Western Cultural Captivity* (Downers Grove, IL: InterVarsity Press, 2009), 98.

19 Rah, *The Next Evangelicalism*, 84.

20 Dallas Willard, "Studies in the Book of Apostolic Acts: Journey into the Spiritual Unknown," unpublished study guide available only from the author. Quoted in Richard J. Foster, *Celebration of Discipline: The Path to Spiritual Growth* (New York: Harper & Row, 1988), 189.

class, race, age, economic, and personality. This inclusive community does not demand everyone be analogous to be loved and accepted; nor does it require people to change their essential strengths and natural talents to fit together. Lions are still lions; lambs are still lambs. This community celebrates diversity and learns to live together without devaluing or destroying the other members of the community.

Safe Refuge

The second ecclesial value of Wesleyan-Holiness urban communities is safe refuge. Kingdom communities must be places of spiritual, emotional, and physical protection that promote *shalom*. If a person visited a zoo and saw an exhibit sign that read, "Lion-Lamb Enclosure," there would be no lambs and several overweight lions. Darwinian theories of biological evolution assert that the strong get stronger and the weak get eaten. Such is the cultural environment in which we live. However, for urban communities to be Christian, they must be based on relationships where natural instincts give way to new desires. Christian communities must learn new ways to live together that do not intentionally hurt or harm the other.

Lion-like people learn, by the power of the Holy Spirit, to live without the taste of blood in their mouths. They begin to use their naturally powerful personalities to reinforce and strengthen the community, rather than to destroy or divide it. In a not-so-subtle allusion to the new creation, Isaiah says that "the lion will eat straw like the ox" (11:7). This community of God's people is a place where lions become trustworthy, where lambs are protected, and where new ways of coexistence are explored to sustain life together without taking life from one another. Mildred Wynkoop describes the nature of the safety in Christian fellowship that *agape* provides: "The fellowship of goodwill and freedom from vindictiveness and underhanded intrigue in a community of persons whose temperaments, ideals, goals, and cultural biases are at sharp odds with each other, is the kind of thing that is amazing and winsome."[21]

The use of power is an essential part of becoming a safe community. All power must be wielded for the good of the whole. Robert Linthicum defines power as "the ability, capacity, and willingness of a person, a group of people or an

---

21 Mildred Bangs Wynkoop, *A Theology of Love: The Dynamic of Wesleyanism* (Kansas City, MO: Beacon Hill Press of Kansas City, 1972), 41.

institution to act."[22] The ability, capacity, and willingness to act are constructive or destructive based on how they are used. Linthicum suggests that there are two essential types of power: unilateral and relational.[23] Unilateral power is power over another person or group of people and, if not kept in check, can degenerate quickly into dominating power that is exercised with force and fear. Relational power is not power *over* another; it is power *with* another that is both mutual and reciprocal. The foundation of relational power is based on respect, a belief in the basic dignity of the other, and the kingdom conviction that every person has something to offer to the community. Donald Dayton alludes to a Wesleyan egalitarianism that views the atonement as for all, without distinction of status or class. Dayton says that if this were not true, then—as Wesley forewarned—"the character of grace may be at stake."[24]

Dietrich Bonhoeffer confronted the concern about power when he wrote, "Every Christian community must realize that not only do the weak need the strong, but also the strong cannot exist without the weak. The elimination of the weak is the death of the fellowship."[25] This understanding of Christian community promotes a kind of interdependence where justice is measured by the power given to the weakest in the community. Wesleyan ecclesiology maintains that the strong need the weak and the weak need the strong. Wesley insisted that "true religion does not go from the strong to the weak, but from the weak to the strong."[26] When power is mutual and reciprocal it is empowering to all. Ministry in the urban context will model this interdependence in the body of Christ.

Authentic Life Transformation

The third ecclesial value of Wesleyan-Holiness urban communities reflected in Isaiah 11 is authentic life transformation. No matter how much a church desires to be inclusive and safe, it cannot happen unless its members are being genuinely changed. Transformation, in the Christian sense, is not the metamorphosis of

---

22 Linthicum, *Transforming Power*, 81.

23 Linthicum, *Transforming Power*, 81–83.

24 Donald Dayton, "Liberation Theology in the Wesleyan and Holiness Tradition," *Online Journal of Public Theology*, 7.

25 Dietrich Bonhoeffer, *Life Together: The Classic Exploration of Christian Community* (New York: HarperCollins, 1954), 94.

26 John Wesley, *Journal* (May 25, 1786), in *The Works of the Rev. John Wesley, A.M.*, ed. Thomas Jackson (London: Wesleyan Methodist Book Room, 1872; reprinted Grand Rapids: Baker Book House, 1979), 21:466.

lions to lambs but a spiritual transformation of each person into the likeness of Christ. It is a change of nature—not from the essence of who a person is but of taking the very best, God-given aspects of who they are and sanctifying them for kingdom purposes.

To further expand Isaiah's metaphor, whenever lions lose the taste of blood in their mouths, they require a major reorientation of life. This reorientation can be explained as nothing short of conversion and newness of life. It is the difference between being *only* a lion and being a Christ-centered, Spirit-filled lion that God can use for his glory. In a powerful analysis of the improbable rise of the early church, Alan Kreider contends:

> Christian communities worked to transform the habitus of those who were candidates for membership—tinkering with their wiring, or even attempting a more far-reaching rewiring—by two means: catechesis, which rehabituated the candidates' behavior by means of teaching and relationship (apprenticeship); and worship, the communities' ultimate counterformative act, in which the new habitus was enacted and expressed with bodily eloquence. The communities were able to attempt this rewiring because something had happened in the lives of the candidates.[27]

Kreider's description of how catechumens[28] were shaped into disciples indicates that the rehabituation of behaviors and the bodily counterformation of Christian worship were both dependent on the fact that real conversion had taken place in the hearts of the first Christians. Only through personal, individual transformations can a collective Christian community be formed.

There is a vast difference between a collection of individuals and a community of faith. Life transformation is ultimately the distinguishing factor between ordinary community and Christian community. While this transformation involves both divine and human activity, it proceeds first and foremost from the heart of the God. Tod Bolsinger could hardly be more specific when he says that "the *essence* of God is the love that is shared by the Persons of the Trinity, demonstrated in Jesus Christ and poured into our hearts by the Holy Spirit—and that love,

---

27 Alan Kreider, *The Patient Ferment of the Early Church: The Improbable Rise of Christianity in the Roman Empire* (Grand Rapids: Baker Academic, 2016), 41.

28 The term "catechumen" denotes a person preparing to be baptized through rigorous instruction and careful discipleship.

when expressed by the communion of believers, transforms."[29] Authentic life transformation in specific urban communities of faith will precede the authentic transformation of urban communities universally.

Healing and Wholeness

The fourth ecclesial value of Wesleyan-Holiness urban communities implicit in Isaiah 11 is healing and wholeness. The reality of Isaiah's symbolism submits that there will be many lions and lambs entering the church with deep wounds, brokenness, and in desperate need of healing and wholeness. Not all of these wounds will be inflicted on them by others; some will be the self-inflicted consequences of bad decisions and poor choices. No matter how those hurts are derived, all need a welcoming community that will surround them with grace and offer hope in their despair.

The transformation of persons includes a very real element of healing. Ultimately, *shalom* is as much well-being as it is salvation, and salvation is more than forgiveness; it is freedom to begin the journey toward wholeness. This idea is not a false triumphalism that ignores the authentic struggles and suffering of people. Cities are filled with people who are wrestling with all-consuming addictions and debilitating brokenness. There is no place in the urban context for attitudes of superiority, ideological pride, or smug platitudes about spiritual victories. Rather, the journey toward wholeness begins in confronting the personal struggle and the systemic evils that contribute to the brokenness of people and society. Soong-Chan Rah observes that "the tendency to view the holistic work of the church as the action of the privileged toward the marginalized often derails the real work of true community healing. Ministry in the urban context, acts of justice, and racial reconciliation require a deeper engagement with the other—an engagement that acknowledges suffering rather than glossing it over."[30] Wesleyan-Holiness theology can help balance the triumphalism of the prosperity gospel and the worship of success through the necessary corrective brought by stories of struggle and suffering friends.[31]

---

29 Tod E. Bolsinger, *It Takes a Church to Raise a Christian: How the Community of God Transforms Lives* (Grand Rapids: Brazos Press, 2004), 10.

30 Soong-Chan Rah, *Prophetic Lament: A Call for Justice in Troubled Times* (Downers Grove, IL: InterVarsity Press, 2015), 154.

31 Rah, *Prophetic Lament*, 154.

Brokenness and destructive behavior are often the results of isolation from a caring community. Bonhoeffer reminds us, "Sin demands to have a man by himself. It withdraws him from the community. The more isolated a person is, the more destructive will be the power of sin over him, and the more deeply he becomes involved in it, the more disastrous is his isolation."[32] In the loneliness of city life, Wesleyan-Holiness communities invite people into accountable relationships where they can be rescued from the dangerous waters of isolation and brought into the healing flow of grace. The church fulfills its mission when it is a hospital for sinners, not a museum for saints. The record of the first Christians indicates that those outside of the *koinonia* were attracted by the way the Christians obediently loved one another, as Jesus commanded them to do before his death (John 13:34). "It remains true today that a lot of people understand the gospel by what they see in church communities. . . . Where there is love for God and one another, the gospel is an embodied reality."[33]

Christian Community

The four aspects of Christian community set forth in Isaiah's vision are a snapshot of the already, but not yet, kingdom of God. Inclusive diversity, safe refuge, life transformation, and healing community are the seeds of heaven on earth. This vision is not possible through human ingenuity and striving. Isaiah prophesies that it is only possible because God has raised up "the Root of Jesse" (11:10), providing the enabling grace to live that way. The messianic prophecy foretells that Jesus of Nazareth is the Branch who brings new life out of death.

The life of the Trinity creates, sustains, and renews this community and its members more and more into the likeness of the new Adam. Alan Roxburgh and Fred Romanuk state, "The One who encounters us in Jesus is the God who is relationship as Father, Son, and Spirit. God called into being a creation that reflects God's nature. In the New Testament and in the early church, this meant forming a people in a new community that reflected in its life together the nature of God. The church was the sign, witness, and foretaste of God's life in the future of all creation."[34]

---

32 Bonhoeffer, *Life Together*, 112.
33 Henry H. Knight III and F. Douglas Powe, Jr., *Transforming Community: The Wesleyan Way to Missional Congregations* (Nashville: Discipleship Resources, 2016), Kindle Location 434.
34 Alan J. Roxburgh and Fred Romanuk, *The Missional Leader: Equipping Your Church to Reach a Changing World* (San Francisco: Jossey-Bass, 2006), 123.

The task of Wesleyan-Holiness church planters and pastors is to invite the people of God to live into the new creation of God by pointing to the vision, modeling the lifestyle, and "cultivating an environment in which this relationality of the kingdom might be experienced."[35] Isaiah's eschatological vision teaches us that human beings are hope-shaped creatures, which means that how we live today is completely shaped by what we believe about our future. "God's future is not in a plan or strategy that [one] introduces; it is _among_ the people of God."[36] This hopeful future must be aligned with a Wesleyan-Holiness ecclesiology for the city.

A Church for the City
Bronx Bethany Church of the Nazarene (New York)

In the early 1960s, a small group of Jamaican nationals migrated to the United States and settled in the Bronx in New York City. They searched for a church where they could worship with a familiar theology and liturgy but were rejected as members because of their race. They eventually formed their own congregation, and on the recommendation of their first pastor, Rev. V. Seymour Cole, they joined the Church of the Nazarene in 1964. In 2000, Rev. Dr. Samuel Vassel came from Jamaica to serve as their second pastor, which he did until he was elected to serve New York City as a district superintendent in the Church of the Nazarene.

Now, more than fifty years later, the congregation is being led by only its third pastor, Rev. Richard Griffiths, who was himself raised in the Bronx Bethany church. As a Jamaican-American who immigrated with his family when he was five, Pastor Rich is in a unique position to teach people, as he says, how to live _in_ Babylon while also leading people in ministry _to_ Babylon.

Early in the church's history they acquired a building on East 227th Street, near where many of the founding members lived. Rev. Cole, the founding pastor, took seriously the church's role in the neighborhood, helping initiate the 47th Precinct Clergy Coalition to increase relationships between neighborhood and law enforcement. One of the city's largest housing projects is just a block away from the church building. The familiar cycles of poverty and crime have perpetuated distrust and violence in the area, causing many of the Jamaican families who

---

35 Roxburgh and Romanuk, _The Missional Leader_, 123.
36 Roxburgh and Romanuk, _The Missional Leader_, 145. Emphasis added.

were charter members of the church to relocate into suburban neighborhoods as they became more upwardly mobile. With options to relocate, the church chose to remain in the neighborhood with the intent of being a force of change.

In 2005 Pastors Publio and Martha Fajardo joined Bronx Bethany as pastors to the growing Latino community surrounding the church. As Colombian immigrants themselves, they have worked hard to develop relationships among the many different Spanish-speaking cultures present in the area. Led by Pastor Martha since her husband's death, the Latino worship service and ministry have seen slow and steady growth over the last fifteen years, and they now are a significant part of the Bronx Bethany Church.

But it is not easy to bring unity among people who come from such different cultures, languages, and life experiences. Although Bronx Bethany began out of its own founders' experiences of bigotry and exclusion, Pastor Rich admits that people are not always aware of how one's own culture can be discriminatory against another's. He is intentional about unifying the two groups as one congregation, asking how they can create space for one another without perpetuating the harm of tokenism that both groups have experienced in the past. The fruit of this hard work is evidenced not only in Bronx Bethany but also in the beginnings of three church plants in Colombia as a result of Bronx Bethany's investment in leaders who have returned to plant churches in their home country.

It seems that church planting is part of Bronx Bethany's DNA. Pastor Rich helped launch a new church in New York City several years before becoming lead pastor of Bronx Bethany, and the church is now prayerfully considering other planting opportunities. Though there are many congregations throughout New York City, Pastor Rich recognizes there are few who share the same theological foundation of the Wesleyan-Holiness tradition. And, he says, the work to which we give ourselves depends on our missional understanding of who we are. "The way we manage properties, our heritage, and new church-planting opportunities—all of these things come out of our way of understanding how to be missional people in the Bronx."

For Reflection or Discussion

1. Where have you experienced a community that practiced inclusive diversity, or one that practiced exclusive selectivity? What processes, practices, or values were at work to make a community diverse and inclusive or exclusive and selective?

2. Reflect again on the Soong-Chan Rah quote from this chapter: "The tendency to view the holistic work of the church as the action of the privileged toward the marginalized often derails the real work of true community healing. Ministry in the urban context, acts of justice, and racial reconciliation require a deeper engagement with the other—an engagement that acknowledges suffering rather than glossing it over." How do you respond? What from your own life experience confirms or challenges this statement?

3. If justice is indeed measured by the power given to the weakest in the community, how just is your current church community? What practices, values, and systems does a community need to cultivate an interdependence between strong and weak?

City Practice
Visit a Recovery Group

There are few places that embody safety, inclusivity, transformation, and healing like a Celebrate Recovery or AA/NA group. Find out where the nearest meeting is and contact a leader to ask permission to visit and observe. Explain why you want to observe, and make it clear that you will not be taking notes or otherwise documenting the meeting in any way. Many of these groups are private and closed, with good reason, so if they deny your request, accept the decision graciously and move on. If you find a group willing to allow a visitor, make plans to attend and observe at least three times. As you listen, notice what elements or structures are in place to create and maintain the culture. What similarities do you see between this group and the passage in Isaiah 11? What similarities or differences do you see between this recovery group and a typical church service? Consider how a church culture could learn from and incorporate some of the foundational elements of a recovery group. You may even want to sit down with the leader(s) of the group to find out more.

PART 3
STRATEGY & PRACTICE

Having explored the context and history of the work of the Church of the Nazarene in the city in Part 1, and having laid the theological foundation of Wesleyan-Holiness spirituality and ecclesiology in Part 2, we now look in Part 3 at the very real challenges, possibilities, and potential of an urban future for the church.

6

CHALLENGES TO AN URBAN FUTURE

The early Nazarenes' concern for society, affirmation of historic church traditions, regard for education, and tolerance of diverse thinking and practice combined to give them an optimistic view of transformation. These deeply held convictions led them to believe that the culture could be changed by the grace of God. Thus, their twofold missional purpose of spreading scriptural holiness throughout the land, and ministry to and among the poor was not merely a strategy—it was a calling.

However, with the Great Reversal came a different perspective of both the world and the possibilities for real cultural change. Pessimism and fear replaced optimism and hope. Mainstream culture felt threatening to the life of faith. The concern of worldly contamination made early Nazarene leaders apprehensive. As David Moberg points out, "Nazarene leaders who had been strongly sympathetic to the labor movement became antipathetic toward it after World War I. Their social welfare work suffered from steadily increasing neglect. When pronouncements were made on social issues, they were buried in committee reports dealing with church members' standards of personal behavior."[1] When a church struggles

---

1 David O. Moberg, *The Great Reversal: Reconciling Evangelism and Social Concern* (Eugene, OR: Wipf & Stock Publishers, 2006), 30.

to decide whether the gospel has the power to change society or if it is best to be removed from the mess, then cities and the people who live in them become the first casualties.

A 1986 survey among Nazarene pastors and laypersons revealed that one-third of them grew up in a small town and that almost the same percentage were raised in rural areas.[2] Urban ministry strategist David Best observes, "Our denomination [the Church of the Nazarene] was founded in an overwhelmingly rural country but had most of its churches in America's urban areas. Today, the United States is essentially an urbanized nation, but the majority of our churches are in small towns and rural areas."[3] In a report on pastors in the Church of the Nazarene, sociologist Kenneth Crow reported that, by 1996, half of all Nazarene churches and pastors were serving small towns or rural areas.[4] Further, research in 1990 also indicated that three out of five new Nazarene ministers begin their pastoral ministry in rural areas and towns with fewer than ten thousand people.[5]

These numbers are not an indictment against rural areas and small towns, or of the many churches represented there. In so many ways, the church of Jesus Christ is better because of them. But the nurturing of this many church leaders in small towns and the rural heartland contributes to a continued misunderstanding of the city. As long as anti-urban sentiments contradict the affirmation that the whole gospel is for the whole world, the mindset will continue to pervade the thinking of some in the church, causing them to wonder if a return to the cities is worth the investment. The Great Reversal's hegemony is resilient.

This mindset presents a psychological and philosophical challenge for the missional objectives to be accomplished in our great cities. But there are other difficulties. The goal of this chapter will be to consider some of the imminent challenges to an urban future for the church. None of them, by the grace of God, is insurmountable. Yet they must each be named, lest they continue to be unnec-

---

2 Kenneth E. Crow, "The Nazarene Listening Post," paper presented to Association of Nazarene Sociologists and Researchers (1986). Cited in David M. Best, *The Urban Imperative*, unpublished book commissioned by the Church of the Nazarene Mission Strategy, United States/Canada, 15.

3 David M. Best, *The Urban Imperative*, 36.

4 Crow, "The Corps of Pastors of the Church of the Nazarene," paper presented to Association of Nazarene Sociologists and Researchers (1996). Cited in Best, *The Urban Imperative*, 36.

5 Crow, "Clergy Preparation from the Perspective of Recent Additions to the Nazarene Ministerial Corps," paper presented to Association of Nazarene Sociologists and Researchers (1990). Cited in Best, *The Urban Imperative*, 36.

essary barriers to the good work God has prepared for his church in the yet-to-be-fully-explored harvest fields of cities.

Gentrification and Poverty

The term "gentrification" was first introduced in 1964 by Ruth Glass while she studied the housing and social class changes in London. Although her initial analysis of gentrification has been updated by current urban researchers, her observations were groundbreaking to theories of urban development. Gentrification has been defined as "the transformation of a working-class or vacant area of the central city into middle-class residential and/or commercial use."[6] While commercial use is also named, housing occupies the spotlight in most discussions of gentrification.

With the rise of suburbanization and an automobile-focused society, urban dwellers migrated out of urban centers and, in many cases, so did businesses and economic stability. "[The] people who were left in the central cities oftentimes were the ones who were not able to be as mobile. As a result . . . those left in the central cities tended to be lower-income minorities."[7] All of these transitions led to a downward cycle of deterioration of neighborhoods, loss of tax revenue needed to maintain infrastructure, and many residents left without viable job opportunities, adequate education, or even basic amenities.

"Blight" is an economic term that describes the conditions of urban areas that are in disrepair.[8] Colin Gordon suggests that "blight" is not synonymous with "slum" but does refer to conditions that gradually lead to a final condition known as a slum.[9] When an area is considered officially blighted, eminent domain is declared in order to relocate local residents, raze buildings, and invite developers into the revitalization process. Gentrification is typically the end result of the restoration of these deteriorating areas.

Urban missiologist Sean Benesh identifies three significant aspects of modern American cities that have resulted from gentrifying urban cores. First, in efforts

---

6 Loretta Lees, Tom Slater, and Elvin Wyly, *Gentrification* (New York: Routledge, 2008), xv.

7 Sean Benesh, *Exegeting the City: What You Need to Know about Church Planting in the City Today* (Portland: Urban Loft Publishers, 2015), Kindle Location 521.

8 Mark R. Gornik, *To Live in Peace: Biblical Faith and the Changing Inner City* (Grand Rapids: Wm. B. Eerdmans Publishing Co., 2002), 35.

9 Colin Gordon, *Mapping Decline: St. Louis and the Fate of the American City* (Philadelphia: University of Pennsylvania Press, 2008), 190.

to revitalize their urban centers, many cities "are specifically, strategically, and unabashedly throwing their lot in with the creative class," which suggests that the key to many city strategies for revitalization is to encourage gentrification, with the explicit aim of attracting a particular socioeconomic group often referred to as the creative class but also labeled in present-day jargon as "hipsters," "yupsters," or "bohemians."[10]

Second, as deindustrialization brought economic downturn to cities, the new trajectory is "toward a *creative economy*, and how this growing creative class workforce is helping to reshape cities." Cities are reinventing themselves "to attract people who are mobile, white-collar, and have discretionary income."[11] With these new consumers come rejuvenated economic vitality, a renewed tax-revenue stream, and the demand for the kind of infrastructure and lifestyle amenities this socioeconomic group is accustomed to having. Coffee shops, microbreweries, bookstores, and bike paths soon follow. Human geography scholar and gentrification specialist Loretta Lees offers insight into the minds of contemporary city planners: "Urban revitalization strategies are aimed not just at attracting middle-class gentrifiers as resident taxpayers, but also at bringing them back to urban areas as consuming, and in that spending, visitors."[12]

Third, cities are transforming from manufacturing-based economies to knowledge-based economies. The knowledge-based economy is being driven by artists, architects, fashion designers, publishers, and tech start-up companies who value the grittiness and authenticity that the urban core has to offer.[13]

The gentrification effect means that cities are embracing "cultural consumption" as the primary enticement to return to the city.[14] Young professionals are increasingly attracted to the energy, opportunities, racial diversity, and quality of life offered by urban living. As an example, in Baltimore, the number of degree-holding young people living in the urban core increased by 92 percent

---

10 Benesh, *Exegeting the City*, Kindle Location 587.

11 Benesh, *Exegeting the City*, Kindle Location 587.

12 Loretta Lees, "The Ambivalence of Diversity and the Politics of Urban Renaissance: The Case of Youth in Downtown Portland, Maine," *International Journal of Urban and Regional Research* 27, no. 3 (October 13, 2003), 614, http://onlinelibrary.wiley.com/doi/abs/10.1111/1468-2427.00469.

13 Benesh, *Exegeting the City*, Kindle Location 628. The term "artisan-based economies" has also been used to describe what is being referred to here as "knowledge-based economies."

14 Benesh, *Exegeting the City*, Kindle Location 641. Consumer Culture Theory is the sociological study of the consumption choices and behaviors of people to determine values and principles of belief.

between 2000 and 2010.[15] And in Pittsburgh, while the adult population continues to decrease, the percentage of young college graduates grew by 53 percent
from 2000 to 2014—or, almost 15,000.[16]

Gentrification has been helpful in some ways, but it has also brought momen-
tous challenges, such as fostering what George Galster and Jason Booza have
identified as "bipolar neighborhoods," or neighborhoods in which very low- and
very high-income groups live together. Their findings indicate that bipolar
neighborhoods have been on a precipitous rise since 1970 and that, on average,
bipolar neighborhoods have significantly greater shares of high-income families,
racial diversity, higher percentages of middle-aged persons, and an excessively el-
evated number of renters.[17] Middle-income groups are conspicuously absent from
bipolar neighborhoods, creating an even more exaggerated condition of bimodal income distribution.[18] The extreme polarities between the very rich and the
working poor living side by side have not proven to reduce class-based prejudic-
es, nor have they produced upward social mobility for lower-income residents in
close proximity with their financially, if not socially, successful neighbors.[19] Most
of the higher-quality municipal services and retail establishments—for example,
coffee shops and organic grocery stores—that are generated by the presence of
high-income residents are not affordable benefits for the poor even though they
may be geographically accessible.

In his book on the built environment of cities, Eric Jacobsen alleges that gentrification is largely a problem of supply and demand, and he claims that to balance the inequities that currently exist between those with sufficient means and

---

15 Stephanie Hanes, "The New 'Cool' Cities for Millennials," *The Christian Science Monitor*, February 1, 2015, https://www.csmonitor.com/USA/Society/2015/0201/The-new-cool-cities-for-Millennials.

16 Dan Majors, "Pittsburgh's Youth Exodus Reverses: Millennials Are Being Drawn
to the City," *Pittsburgh Post-Gazette*, August 7, 2016, https://www.post-gazette.com/local/
city/2016/08/08/Millennials-are-being-drawn-to-Pittsburgh/stories/201608070226&x-
id=17259,15700023,15700124,15700149,15700168,15700186,15700191,15700201,15700208.

17 George Galster and Jason Booza, "The Rise of the Bipolar Neighborhood," *Journal of the
American Planning Association* 73, no. 4 (Autumn 2007), 421–35. Out of 2,377 neighborhoods in New
York, 705 are considered "bipolar" (29.7 percent); for Los Angeles, 370 of 2,016 neighborhoods qualify
as bipolar (18.4 percent).

18 George Galster and Jason Booza, "The Rise of the Bipolar Neighborhood," *Journal of the
American Planning Association* 73, no. 4 (Autumn 2007), 421–35. Galster and Booza's findings indicate
that the average bipolar neighborhood has a bimodal (if asymmetric) income distribution, with the
lowest- and highest-income groups constituting almost 69 percent of the total.

19 George Galster and Jason Booza, "The Rise of the Bipolar Neighborhood," *Journal of the American Planning Association* 73, no. 4 (Autumn 2007), 421–35.

the working poor all that is needed is to gentrify more urban neighborhoods.[20] While this is an oversimplification of Jacobsen's argument, the fact remains that the issue of inequality requires more than offsetting goods and services provided; it has as much to do with making a living. While the urban centers of many cities are attempting positive change, the vast majority of jobs available to the working poor are located in the suburbs. The cost of doing business has driven a large percentage of companies that typically provide working-class jobs out to the suburbs, leaving mostly restaurants or large corporations in the city. Edward Glaeser reports that about half the jobs in the largest cities in America are now located more than ten miles away from the city center.[21] Furthermore, more than two-thirds of all manufacturing jobs currently take place outside city limits.[22] Thus, Abram Lueders reminds us, many residents of traditional urban neighborhoods are reverse commuters, and—unless one lives in the largest and most dense cities—"American urban life is a fragmented experience."[23]

The long-term effects of gentrification on the urban poor are varied. Those who have been relocated through eminent domain, or who can no longer afford to live in their new economy, have migrated into still-depressed urban or inner-ring suburban neighborhoods. As city cores revitalize through gentrification and the edges of suburbia continue to flourish with new housing, urban sprawl is generated, leaving rings of older, often deteriorating, suburbs of city centers. These inner-ring suburbs are considered to be the first generation of suburbia that developed after World War II.[24] Once newer, nicer, and well appointed for a comfortable way of life, these neighborhoods have also undergone dramatic change. Pete Saunders reports: "From an image standpoint, [inner-ring neighborhoods] lack the vitality and energy of older urban neighborhoods, and they [have] lost much of the neighborly comfort and security that newer suburbs have since acquired. From an economic standpoint, they [have] lost middle-class residents

---

20 Eric O. Jacobsen, *The Space Between: A Christian Engagement with the Built Environment* (Grand Rapids: Baker Academic, 2012), 215–37.

21 Edward Glaeser, *Triumph of the City: How Our Greatest Invention Makes Us Richer, Smarter, Greener, Healthier, and Happier* (New York: Penguin Press, 2011), 177.

22 Alan Ehrenhalt, *The Great Inversion and the Future of the American City* (New York: Vintage Books, 2013), Kindle Location 521.

23 Abram Lueders, "Evangelicals and the New Urbanism," *Marginalia: Los Angeles Review of Books*, April 22, 2017, https://marginalia.lareviewofbooks.org/evangelicals-new-urbanism/.

24 Isabel Wilkerson, *The Warmth of Other Suns: The Epic Story of America's Great Migration* (New York: Random House, 2010), 378. Quoted in Soong-Chan Rah, *Prophetic Lament: A Call for Justice in Troubled Times* (Downers Grove, IL: InterVarsity Press, 2015), 87–88.

as people move closer to the center of the metro area, or farther away. Socially and culturally, they [are] viewed as dated, even obsolete. They [have] lost their luster when luster is what sells homes and communities."[25]

With the intensifying push of gentrification in urban cores, these inner-ring neighborhoods are fast becoming the "catch basins for the migrating urban poor who are no longer in the central city."[26] Lacking basic amenities, such as health care options, libraries, standardized schools, and adequate civic services, many of these sprawling, older inner-ring suburbs are ignored by city planners, lack enforcement of building code laws, and consist of low-density housing, neglected strip malls, unkempt convenience stores, and payday-loan operations.

Studies of church-planting trends over the last fifteen years indicate that a high percentage of new churches were started in the suburbs.[27] The highest percentage of urban church planting is happening in gentrified neighborhoods. Because church planters are, according to Sean Benesh, the creative class of the church, they are naturally drawn to plant churches in these areas.[28] Like-minded artisans and creatives are there, the environment is inviting, and churches are needed just as they are needed in other parts of the city. Yet not all of those in gentrified neighborhoods can be counted among the creative class. Gentrification is an economic conversation and, for Wesleyan-Holiness people, a spiritual one.[29] Decaying urban neighborhoods are not the preferred future of those who have endured the impact of blight and the loss of decent living conditions. In many cases, gentrification has been an improvement. But the side effects of displacement, loss of identity, and unaffordable housing must be addressed—if not by city planners then by the church. Justice begins with mercy.

---

25 Pete Saunders, "Inner Ring Suburbs Could Use Some Attention," *Forbes*, September 28, 2016, https://www.forbes.com/sites/petesaunders1/2016/09/28/inner-ring-suburbs-could-use-some-attention/#43c110eb3b50.

26 Benesh, *Exegeting the City*, Kindle Location 667.

27 Sean Benesh, *Metrospiritual: The Geography of Church Planting* (Eugene, OR: Resource Publications, 2011), 5. The study was based on the research of seven cities in the western half of the United States and Canada.

28 Benesh, *Exegeting the City*, Kindle Location 999.

29 Sean Benesh, "Church Planting in the City," in *Text & Context: Church Planting in Canada in Post-Christendom*, ed. Leonard Hjalmarson (Portland: Urban Loft Publishers, 2013), 187–96.

The Separation of Evangelism and Social Reform

A significant remnant of the residual effects of the Great Reversal is the unwarranted separation between personal evangelism and social reform rooted in the modernist-fundamentalist controversies of the 1920s and '30s. Today this division could be expressed as the conservative-liberal debate. Political conservativism is often linked to evangelical faith and soul-winning; political liberalism is often linked to concerns for the disenfranchised and tax increases for government welfare programs. The first emphasizes the spiritually minded next world; the second emphasizes the physically minded here and now.[30] This false dichotomy has caused some urban ministers to be classified as a special-interest group independent of the real mission of the church. However, from their inception, Wesleyan-Holiness churches have maintained a more holistic, undivided vision of salvation and redemption.

Kenneth Collins reiterates the notion that, in faithfulness to their theological legacy, Wesleyan-Holiness denominations will be marked by two key characteristics. First, a "no-nonsense emphasis on conversion, resulting in a distinctively holy life."[31] Roger Olson corroborates this conviction by adding, "Conversion, regeneration, [and] sanctification are the meat and potatoes of Wesleyanism."[32] Second, "Wesleyans will be characterized by a stress on social action that will be informed not only by the needs of the poor but also by a keen awareness of the danger of riches."[33]

Evangelism and compassion are not mutually exclusive. Wesleyan-Holiness people have a broader theological vision that believes saving a person's soul while ignoring the plight and cause of their suffering is neither just nor Christian. Jesus's first recorded sermon was an announcement of freedom from spiritual captivity and a confrontation of the systems of the world that imprison people who were created in the image of God (Luke 4:18–19). The uniting of both is the message of Jubilee. In the spirit of Jubilee, the Wesleyan-Holiness

---

30 A preoccupation with the next world was the essence of Gnosticism, one of the earliest Christian heresies. The Gospel of John and the Johannine epistles were written, in part, to combat this ideology of separation between the physical and spiritual worlds.

31 Kenneth J. Collins, *Power, Politics, and the Fragmentation of Evangelicalism: From the Scopes Trial to the Obama Administration* (Downers Grove, IL: IVP Academic, 2012), 113.

32 Roger E. Olson, "The World Its Parish: Wesleyan Theology in the Postmodern Global Village," *Asbury Theological Journal* 59, no. 1 (2004), 23.

33 Collins, *Power, Politics, and the Fragmentation of Evangelicalism*, 113.

tradition has a long and fruitful history of both revivalism *and* social reform and, as such, pursues the call to work for the *shalom* of all creation—including the welfare of the city.

National Politics and Social Concerns

Closely related to the unwarranted separation of evangelism and social reform are the political affiliations of a denomination's members. The purpose of the union of three different groups to form the Church of the Nazarene at Pilot Point, Texas, was to promote the biblical doctrine of holiness. At the same time, nearly thirty other prominent groups in the United States held the same conviction. The reason these three groups could merge to form a new denomination while the others did not was based on several shared ideas: the strong affirmation of the ordination of women; a baptismal theology that included infant and believer's baptism without demanding a specific mode of baptism be observed; the willingness to allow for freedom of conscience regarding millennialist theories; a view of divine healing that did not exclude modern medicine; and a shared believers' church ecclesiology.[34] While many other Holiness denominations held exclusive and narrow viewpoints on these issues, the Church of the Nazarene chose to unite Holiness people around middle-way—or *via media*—practices.[35]

An extraordinary aspect of the union at Pilot Point was that the newly formed Church of the Nazarene was able to do what few other evangelical churches were able to achieve in the divisive years that followed the American Civil War: overcome issues of regional politics, prejudice, and the lingering hatred that follows horrific conflict. Names like Bresee, Jernigan, and Reynolds came together from north, south, and east to embrace the transformational idea that Christian holiness could break down any walls of separation. It was a movement of the Holy Spirit rarely seen in post-Civil War America. Stan Ingersol summarizes the miracle of Pilot Point: "The union of churches at Pilot Point was a shining example of the social reality of Christian holiness. At the heart of the Christian message is a word of reconciliation: first between sinners and Divine Love; and second,

---

34 Stan Ingersol, "Born in Hope, Borne Onward in Love," paper presented to the Fraternal Delegates Luncheon, Twenty-ninth General Assembly for the Church of the Nazarene, Indianapolis, June 26, 2017.

35 David A. Busic, "The Point of Pilot Point," *Transform the Globe*, April 13, 2018, https://transformtheglobe.com/2018/04/13/the-point-of-pilot-point/.

among the members of the human family who are estranged from one another. Pilot Point signifies the reality that holiness heals hearts and unites people otherwise driven apart by sin, politics, and conflict."[36] The remarkable capacity to set aside strongly held partisan beliefs for the greater mission of the church meant that, in the earliest days of the Church of the Nazarene, there was an uncommon tolerance for a wide-ranging spectrum of political affiliations. Political orientations were not aligned with specific political parties so much as with the social issues of the day.

Since many early Nazarenes worked with the addicted on Skid Row, they aligned themselves politically as prohibitionists.[37] They believed that alcohol had become the root of social ills—not because they believed drinking to be a sin but because they saw firsthand the destruction of people and families that the abuse of alcohol left in its wake.[38] They stood against alcohol and in solidarity with the people to whom they ministered.

Early Nazarenes were also opposed to child slavery and other forms of low-income impoverishment of those in industrial jobs at the turn of the century.[39] They stood with pro-labor movements, unions, and those fighting for livable wages. Their political orientations were informed by their theological orientation and the mission to which they felt called. This stance was an expression of their doctrine of holiness—there is no personal holiness without social holiness.

For many in the church, the social gospel wars changed that perspective. Nazarenes and other like-minded Wesleyan-Holiness churches began to distance themselves from ideas and agendas that began to be labeled and perceived as "liberal." When Nazarenes moved to the suburbs, they were de facto farther away from urban plight and people in obvious need. As a result, they began to vote based on social policies that benefited their new way of life.[40]

Today, the majority of Nazarenes around the world align with conservative political ideologies. There are often positive reasons for doing so. However, it can

---

36 Ingersol, "Born in Hope, Borne Onward in Love."

37 Floyd Cunningham, ed., Stan Ingersol, Harold E. Raser, and David P. Whitelaw, *Our Watchword and Song: The Centennial History of the Church of the Nazarene* (Kansas City, MO: Beacon Hill Press of Kansas City, 2009), Kindle Locations 1548–61, 4573.

38 Tom Nees, *The Holiness Social Ethic and Nazarene Urban Ministry*, doctoral thesis (Wesley Theological Seminary, 1976), 40.

39 B. F. Haynes, "Reformation Versus Transformation," *Herald of Holiness* [now *Holiness Today*] (March 12, 1913), 4. Cited by Nees, *The Holiness Social Ethic and Nazarene Urban Ministry*, 31–32.

40 Cunningham et al., *Our Watchword and Song*, Kindle Locations 7141–7220.

also create tension with urbanites who take a different political position, especially related to areas of social concern.[41] Evangelicalism, particularly in the United States, has often been more closely associated with the fundamentalist-leaning Religious Right and the accompanying temptation to wed nationalism with faith. This alluring temptation must be resisted by Wesleyan-Holiness people—whose first allegiance is to Christ; they must steadfastly challenge any reading of Scripture or cultural ethic that would undermine faithfulness to the middle way that holds evangelism and compassion in proper tension. As William Kostlevy points out, "Neo-fundamentalist historical categories distort the character of evangelicalism and, more significantly, obscure the important links between historic perfectionistic revivalism and . . . twentieth-century reform movements."[42] The impact of Wesleyan-Holiness churches in the urban context will be partially determined by how well they can hold in balance national politics and the work of the kingdom of God.

The Culture of Affluence

The cardinal Wesleyan belief that the poor are a means of grace is one remedy to the middle-class ethos that now permeates much of the Church of the Nazarene in the United States. Stan Ingersol remarks, "The culture of affluence insulates middle-class people in the Western world from the poor." He then ponders, "Has affluence posed the truest test of our Christian character? Is the real crisis over holiness theological in nature, or is it, instead, the temptation to selfishness and a failure of costly discipleship?"[43]

Reflecting on his own denomination, Bishop Kenneth Carder laments that the poor are absent from most local churches and ecclesial structures and that, when they are visible, they are treated more as objects of charity than as friends who

---

41 In a recent survey, American Nazarene clergy were polled regarding their political positions. Two-thirds of those surveyed indicated they were opposed to big government and had no desire to see it "more actively engaged in solving social problems." Further, 87 percent of these ministers identified themselves as politically conservative, 10 percent as moderate, and 4 percent as liberal. Corwin E. Smidt, ed., *Pulpit and Politics: Clergy in American Politics at the Advent of the Millennium* (Waco, TX: Baylor University Press, 2004), 174, 177.

42 William Kostlevy, *Holiness Manuscripts: A Guide to Sources Documenting the Wesleyan Holiness Movement in the United States and Canada* (Chicago: American Theological Library Association, 1994), 40. Quoted in Kenneth Collins, *Power, Politics, and the Fragmentation of Evangelicalism*, 114.

43 Stan Ingersol, *Past and Prospect: The Promise of Nazarene History* (Eugene, OR: Wipf and Stock, 2014), 18.

can help guide the affluent to a closer identification with Jesus. He calls this "a profound theological and ecclesial crisis for United Methodism." Carder's remedy to the crisis is to rediscover the poor as a means of grace: "Renewed relationships with the impoverished may be the means of evangelizing the affluent and breaking the idolatrous grip of the consumerist market logic to which middle-class North American Methodism has fallen captive."[44] Modern urban dwellers often talk about compassion in sentimental and trendy ways, but Wesleyan-Holiness theology calls for the kind of engagement that is mutually beneficial to spiritual formation.

The Complexity of Social Systems

The first Nazarenes engaged in the intertwined endeavors of personal and social transformation. Holistic in theology and practice, urban ministry among the early Nazarenes led to a pattern of comprehensive social ministries and political engagement that was the "most distinctive (and perhaps *defining*) characteristic of early Nazarene urban presence."[45] Their fearless, if not audacious, engagement with the complexities of the systems and structures of urban society were directly related to their experience of perfect love and hopeful optimism in the power of the gospel to transform. The first General Assemblies of the fledgling denomination established entities to reflect their ultimate concerns. A General Orphanage Board and General Board of Social Welfare were inaugurated between 1911 and 1919.[46] Denominational periodicals also reflected the commitment of the church to social reform ministries, including rescue homes for unwed mothers, orphanages, storefront missions, and family-oriented congregations designed to minister to the urban poor.[47]

It was not long before the focus turned from a broad commitment to social change to a narrower concentration on individual, evangelistic soul-winning. Historians note several factors that contributed to this shift, including a growing segment of Nazarene bourgeoisie, the influence of *laissez-faire* religious tenden-

---

44 Kenneth L. Carder, "What Difference Does Knowing Wesley Make?" in *Rethinking Wesley's Theology for Contemporary Methodism*, ed. Randy L. Maddox (Nashville: Kingswood Books, 1998), 30.

45 Stan Ingersol, "Nazarenes and the Urban Ethos: An Exploratory Essay," paper presented to Association of Nazarene Sociologists and Researchers, 1986.

46 Ingersol, "Nazarenes and the Urban Ethos."

47 Nees, "Social Concerns of the Church of the Nazarene During its Formative Years (1895–1920) as Reflected in Its Official Publications," in *The Holiness Social Ethic and Nazarene Urban Ministry*.

cies, and a diminishing national economy.[48] As Nazarenes became more middle class in social standing and more influenced by a rural mindset, denominational institutions were progressively shaped by middle-class values that became increasingly suspicious of the cultural complexity of cities that felt threatening to family ideals. Closely related, the entrepreneurial spirit inextricably bound with the first Nazarenes eventually began to reflect the spirit of the day's business practices and commercial enterprises.[49] As the economy of the nation began to suffer in the Great Depression,[50] funding for expensive ministries began to wane, resulting in less support for social impact ministries.[51]

Those in the rural-Holiness tradition were similarly engaged in social ministries, but their understanding of the solutions to societal evils differed from their urban-Holiness counterparts. They were more apt to focus on issues of personal morality, offering ministries of mercy to individuals they believed were suffering as a result of personal sins and bad decisions. This is illustrated in an account of Johnny Jernigan, related by Stan Ingersol, called "A Long Night in the Slums."[52]

Involved with the Nazarene Rest Cottage in Pilot Point, Texas, and later as the founder of a home for unwed mothers in Bethany, Oklahoma, Jernigan boarded a train for Little Rock, Arkansas. Once there, she confronted the matron of a brothel and took one of the young women back to the Nazarene home in Bethany to be cared for and rehabilitated. Ingersol indicates that this incident was paradigmatic of the changing mindset of the rural-Holiness tradition regarding social reform in the cities. "Her solution for the victims of urban decay was straightforward; it was *a strategy of extraction*."[53] While this was a noble and courageous act of compassion on Jernigan's part, there appeared to be no interest in or attempt to address the social and cultural values that had, at some level, created a market for prostitution; neither was there any effort to confront or reform the civil and political systems that abetted prostitution or kept women from working as prostitutes. It was a strategy to remove a person from the environment of sin but not to change the environment itself.

---

48 Ingersol, *Past and Prospect*, 18.
49 Ingersol, "Nazarenes and the Urban Ethos."
50 The Great Depression originated in the United States and, by most estimates, lasted from 1929 until 1941.
51 Ingersol, "Nazarenes and the Urban Ethos."
52 Ingersol, "Nazarenes and the Urban Ethos."
53 Ingersol, "Nazarenes and the Urban Ethos." Emphasis added.

By the 1920s and into the '40s, Nazarenes had moved "away from a Wesley-an social activism of its pioneers and instead wedded the holiness message to personal standards."[54] Personal standards and lifestyle adjustments are obviously necessary for the holy life, but any holiness that does not also address the social structures that cause the dysfunction will be limited.

A Church for the City
True Light Church of the Nazarene (Kansas City, MO)

When Rev. Alice Piggee-Wallack relocated to Kansas City for her husband's work, she thought she'd only be there a few years. But now, more than thirty years later, it is evident to Piggee-Wallack that God had other plans. In very short order, she began worshiping with Kansas City First Church of the Naza-rene, decided to follow Jesus, and accepted a call to ministry among the poorest in the city. In her career as a social worker she recognized the need to connect with people's spirituality in order to walk them out of poverty, and in 1998 she launched a new church with that mission in mind.

For several years Piggee-Wallack and her congregation shared space with oth-ers while attempting to serve the poorest communities. While ministering out of Beacon Hill Church of the Nazarene, Pastor Alice and her seminary student volunteers walked along several urban blocks to visit with prostitutes, drug deal-ers, and others on the street during the day. They gave out cold drinks, struck up conversations, and developed relationships.

When a former liquor warehouse went up for sale around the corner, Pastor Alice knew it was their place. After it was purchased and renovated, it became the permanent home of True Light Church of the Nazarene, offering refuge and resource in the midst of an otherwise troubled part of the city. After receiving grant funding a few years later, the True Light congregation was able to purchase another property across the street and expand its nutrition, food, and clothing services through the True Light Family Resources Center.

As a black female pastor, Piggee-Wallack has been uniquely positioned to hear the stories and receive the trust of her neighborhood's diverse population—par-ticularly homeless women. In 2006, True Light launched the Emancipation Sta-tion, a women's day shelter with activities, resources, and groups to help women

---

54 Ronald R. Emptage, "Denominational Identity in Historical Perspective," paper presented to Association of Nazarene Sociologists and Researchers, 1989.

gain work and housing. In 2010, they opened Freedom House, a transitional home nearby, to help to prepare homeless single women for a life of independence and self-sufficiency.

Once an area of darkness and hopelessness, the presence of True Light has offered the area of 31st and Charlotte in Kansas City a beacon of love, hope, and healing. The church is an odd and wonderful mix of racial identity and socioeconomic standing—homeless, working people, some who cannot work, and seminary students—all together in a neighborhood that still is not entirely safe. There is somewhat of a revolving door in the congregation, but Pastor Alice takes that as a good sign. "We've gotten very good at sending people," she says cheerfully. "We want to receive people as part of the congregation, but we see people go when they get stability in their lives." This sending includes the seminary graduates, whom Pastor Alice names with pride, and whose lives and ministries have been profoundly shaped by the people of True Light Church of the Nazarene.

For Reflection or Discussion

1. How have you witnessed a spirit of pessimism and fear about cities and/or changing culture, and what have been the effects? Where do you see evidence of those who are exhibiting signs of optimism and hope instead?

2. Busic says in this chapter, "When a church struggles to decide whether the gospel has the power to change society or if it is best to be removed from the mess, then cities and the people who live in them become the first casualties." What factors contribute to the decision to remove ourselves from the mess or to be a transforming presence within it?

3. Considering the progression of urban development—blight, gentrification, and bipolar neighborhoods—how might the presence of a church be an agent of healing and wholeness in a changing neighborhood?

City Practice
Study the City

Unless we are part of the discussions of urban planning and development, most city dwellers don't get to see the big picture of city change. But there is a surprising amount of information available if you know where to look and what questions to ask. Set aside some time to research your own city, looking for blighted areas, inner- and outer-ring neighborhoods, signs of gentrification, and bipolar neighborhoods. Nothing beats being physically present in these areas to learn what's going on, but you can also get information from a city council or chamber of commerce.

7

REVERSING THE
GREAT REVERSAL

The Great Reversal is a part of Nazarene history and, in some measure, part of the history of the broader Wesleyan-Holiness family. Its impact on the relationship between the church and the city cannot be ignored or minimized. This chapter will briefly suggest strategic direction and recommendations for ongoing ministry in the urban context to reverse the Great Reversal.

Function Precedes Form

The question of *function* considers the desired outcomes of church planting, development, and renewal; the question of *form* suggests the creation of systems needed to sustain this work. The guiding concern for both form and function must always be the unique contribution that the Wesleyan-Holiness tradition can bring to the urban context. Mission trumps models. Churches must fashion unique approaches to ministry in the city and not be bound by the tyranny of duplicating other models, regardless of their origin or historical level of success. Knowledge of best practices in urban settings can certainly be helpful, but, as Jim Copple observes, "Because programs and projects are highly contextualized, replications . . . are doomed to failure."[1] Developed ministries should arise from each local context while remaining faithful to Wesleyan-Holiness fundamentals. Urban specialist Michael Mata refers to this approach as "exegeting the commu-

---

1 Jim Copple, personal email to author, October 12, 2015.

nity."[2] Another way to approach ministry development in a localized context is to ask a question: What does your mission field need?

Because cities are dynamic organisms, ministry methods and strategies must be flexible to make contextual adjustments. Many urban church-planting strategies and goals emanate from a church-growth-movement perspective, as Michael R. Jones notes, "emphasizing a social science approach in the tradition of Donald McGavran and C. Peter Wagner."[3] The social science strategy is often inadequate because urban areas change shape and form depending on the transient population living there at any given time. The concept of a toolbox may be a better approach.

Employing a toolbox metaphor, seasoned urban pastor David Best has designed "essentials tools for effective urban ministry."[4] His recommended tools are organized into three categories, with their component parts: (1) *knowledge*— Scripture, classic theology, biblical foundations of urban mission, evangelism, urban spirituality, and corporate spiritual formation; (2) *skills*—exegeting the city to understand its history, social, economic, and political systems, community organizing, reading culture, intercultural diversity, and organizational development/management skills related to nonprofits, boards, building issues, and finances; and (3) *attitudes*—open to diversity, cooperation, collaboration, solidarity with the poor (referring to an incarnational attitude—ministering with presence, not paternalism), and patience.[5]

In 1996, Multicultural Ministries for the Church of the Nazarene convened a meeting of urban missional practitioners. The committee developed core competencies necessary for anyone involved in Nazarene urban church planting. Even though the core competencies were advanced more than twenty years ago, they continue to highlight the qualities needed from urban ministry leaders:

---

2 Michael Mata, "Organizational Leadership in Urban Contexts," seminar, Fuller Theological Seminary (Pasadena, CA, July 13–17, 2015).

3 Michael R. Jones, "Book Review: *Urban Ministry: The Kingdom, the City, and the People of God* by Conn and Ortiz," in *What Does the Text Say: Biblical Studies, Theology, and Pastoral Ministry*, blog, April 24, 2012, https://michaelrjones.wordpress.com/2012/04/24/book-review-urban-ministry-the-kingdom-the-city-the-people-of-god-by-conn-ortiz/.

4 David M. Best, *Successfully Serving the City*, audiobook (Nashville: Towel and Basin and Highley Music Company, 1997).

5 Best, *Successfully Serving the City*.

- an ability to analyze social, economic, and political systems, and to organize appropriate ministry responses
- an ability to develop organizational and financial strategies to create and sustain ministry opportunities
- an ability to analyze and organize a congregation/community for holistic and community-based evangelism
- an understanding of culture, ethnicity, religion, and gender within the urban context
- an ability to develop strategies for working with diverse cultural groups and developing multicultural ministries and leadership
- a clear understanding of biblical and theological themes and paradigms that inform and shape ministry in the city
- a clear understanding of the development of personal leadership skills and spiritual formation.[6]

Although cities are in a constant state of flux, urban pastors must be adaptable and prepared to stay for the long term. Says Best, "The nonnegotiables for such preparation are that it is in *context*, offering relevant *content* and producing the *competencies* that can be measurably demonstrated." Such preparation will require more than new structures. As Best advocates, it "will require new ways of thinking from what most have come to believe about church."[7]

Ecclesial Leadership and Denominational Culture

A denominational urban strategy for the future must be a shared vision. A top-down strategy that is disconnected from the grassroots and from those actually involved in frontline ministry will be counterproductive. Leadership can describe the need and opportunities for ministry in urban centers but must also be willing to learn from the practitioners and to provide the structures through which people are given an opportunity to serve.

Among the indispensable partners for church development in the Church of the Nazarene are district superintendents. District superintendents are the missional and administrative overseers who serve a geographic grouping of churches. Tom Nees comments: "In the Nazarene connectional structure (in the

---

6 David M. Best, *The Urban Imperative*, unpublished book commissioned by the Church of the Nazarene Mission Strategy, United States/Canada, 81.

7 Best, *The Urban Imperative*, 82.

United States and Canada at least), nothing gets traction for church development without the support of district superintendents. I think district superintendents serving in urban areas would welcome the opportunity to engage in collaborative strategic planning. They would likely welcome the opportunity to develop and implement a visionary and workable strategy."[8]

The late Jesse Miranda, founder and one-time CEO of the National Hispanic Christian Leadership Conference, suggested that there are certain characteristics and qualities in district superintendents that are critical for urban leadership development and church planting:

> Affirm pastors where they are with the gifts they have; recognize that growth in urban contexts takes time; [urban] church plant-ing is not like a factory, but a garden; sometimes be operative in leadership style—doing something to get it done—but often, [leadership style] needs to function cooperatively; utilize splits and divisions [of churches] with [the] surgical precision of separating Siamese twins to begin new works; plan ahead—view differences as possibilities; [cultivate an] attitude and skill that can convert a problem into potential.[9]

Go back and reread the characteristics and qualities that are necessary for urban churches to thrive. Several of the statements could be written down and placed where those who shepherd pastors can see them often.

Even as district superintendents must share an urban vision, so frontline urban mission entrepreneurs need to be encouraged, recognized, and supported. Networks for urban ministry practitioners should be promoted and nurtured. It is possible that the urban ministry of the future will emerge from loyal mavericks who function best outside the box of institutional expectations and control. If the Wesleyan-Holiness tradition desires a vital future in the urban context, its district leadership must inspire, embrace, and incarnate the vision. Less control can be unsettling and messy, but life in the city is messy. There are plenty of churches that have messes, and mess alone does not make them part of a move-ment. But there is no such thing as a movement that is not messy. Leadership in urban contexts must grow comfortable with discomfort.

---

8 Tom Nees, personal email to author, October 2015.
9 Jesse Miranda, interview, cited in Best, *The Urban Imperative*, 79.

Leadership development also is critical for the sustainability of urban church planting, development, and renewal. Wesleyan-Holiness universities and seminaries could develop courses that focus on the city, including excursions into city life and community-mapping exercises. "Training urban leaders is done best in the city. . . . Context always affects the content, interpretation, and application of what we are learning."[10] With astounding prescience, the great urban missiologist Harvie Conn discerned the changing cultural dynamics around cities and maintained that "an urban world required not suburban theological and missionary education with a class on the city, but 'training in the cities. And training that combines the study with the street, that teaches people to move easily from the books to the barrios.'"[11]

This kind of immersion into the richness of the urban context would affirm the diversity in demographics and ethnic cultures. Leadership development in urban areas would include support for ministerial preparation among ethnic minorities. Denominational resources could also be distributed to support the development of immigrant ministries.

The Necessity of Ecumenical Partnerships

Making a significant impact on any great metropolitan area will require intentional cooperation with other churches, denominations, and other cultural institutions, i.e., community development partners. Tim Keller submits, "No one kind of church—no one church model or theological tradition—can reach an entire city."[12] Wesley's emphasis on a catholic spirit recognizes that other theological traditions have important perspectives to share with those with a Wesleyan-Holiness affinity, and can offer multiple ways to benefit a shared mission.

While denominational distinctions are multifaceted, much can be gained from working together. "As much as we want to believe that most people will want to become our particular kind of Christian, it is not true. The city will not be won unless many different denominations become dynamic mini-movements."[13]

---

10 Best, *The Urban Imperative*, 79.

11 Harvie M. Conn, newsletter, December 1983. Quoted in Mark R. Gornik, "The Legacy of Harvie M. Conn," *International Bulletin of Mission Research* Vol. 35, No. 4 (October 2011), 213, http://www.internationalbulletin.org/issues/2011-04/2011-04-212-gornik.html#_ednref15.

12 Timothy Keller, *Center Church: Doing Balanced, Gospel-Centered Ministry in Your City* (Grand Rapids: Zondervan, 2012), 368.

13 Keller, *Center Church*, 369.

Whereas a local church can change a neighborhood, only a unified movement can change an entire city. For this reason, Keller further maintains that, to make a real difference in a city, one church for every thousand people would be the tipping point to do more than simply maintain but actually *grow* the body of Christ. "The relationship of the number of churches to churchgoing people is exponential, not linear."[14]

A good deal can be learned from the success of sister denominations. The Church of God (Anderson)'s ministry within African-American communities, the Wesleyan Church's positive influence in helping change unjust immigration policies, and the Salvation Army's success in establishing community development centers are all notable. Church executives could consider the possibility for denominations to combine their strengths and weaknesses to produce something sustainable in vast urban areas. The Salvation Army is recognized globally for their effectiveness in urban compassionate ministries, but they are not as well known for their local congregations. The Church of the Nazarene and the Salvation Army could potentially work together to establish dynamic works that include the best of both traditions.

With exorbitant real estate costs in urban areas, facilities could be shared as a matter of stewardship. Interdenominational co-pastorates could be considered. Synergy is created when a kingdom mindset prevails over who receives the credit. An experimental beta project in one city could prove to be invaluable for future urban strategies. This is a potential strategic step to move from linear to exponential, incremental to movement. Ministry in the urban context welcomes ecumenical partnerships. Addressing diversity requires innovative approaches and integrated cooperation. The catholic spirit of Wesley, and of those who are his offspring, makes these partnerships not only possible but imperative.

Expect . . . Attempt

Perhaps no academic in the last quarter century has made more of a contribution to urban missiology than Harvie M. Conn. Playing "the role of revivalist" for renewal in the city, his writings, teachings, and persistent example helped birth a

---

14   Keller, *Center Church*, 362–65.

rejuvenated emphasis on urban studies and urban church planting that had been dormant for decades.[15]

In *The American City and the Evangelical Church*, Conn analyzed the history of the church in the American city through the lens of three time frames: 1870–1920, 1920–1970, and 1970–1990. Recounting "the principal target of the early church in its first 300 years was the city," Conn refutes two cynical biases regarding the evangelical church and the American city. First, the anti-urban bias that the city is a stronghold of evil, impious and secular, with no hope for redemption and lift. Second, the greatest opportunities for the church to succeed are more easily achieved in the rural context. With an expressed interest in "the ethno-sociological makeup of the city," Conn contends that the histories of the city and the church in the city are intertwined and cannot be dichotomized into good versus evil. Rather, the gospel in the city must be viewed with a renewed, vibrant potentiality, capable of both evangelical transformation and social reform. In this, Conn was highly supportive of the Wesleyan-Holiness theological emphasis of the transformation of people, systems, and cultures. Conn's contribution to a missiology for the city is profound and abiding. The future of planting, developing, and renewing urban churches is sustained by his prophetic challenge, "Expect great things from God for the city; attempt great things for God in the city."[16]

A Church for the City
Neighbor to Neighbor and Tapestry Church (Raleigh, NC)

In 1989 a small group from North Raleigh First Church of the Nazarene—a predominantly white, upper-middle-class congregation—began a relationship with the predominantly black, low-income community at Walnut Terrace in southeast Raleigh, which was the largest government housing project in the city. After several years of receiving assistance through donated goods, four mothers from Walnut Terrace approached the North Raleigh church members with a searing question: how can we be part of lasting change in our community? In the conversations that followed, it became clear that a new approach was needed

---

15 Gornik, "The Legacy of Harvie M. Conn," 215.

16 Harvie M. Conn, *The American City and the Evangelical Church: A Historical Overview* (Grand Rapids: Baker Books, 1994), 9–11.

to tackle the community members' greatest concerns: afterschool care, positive mentors for children, and adult education to achieve living-wage work.

In response to these needs, Neighbor to Neighbor launched in 1996 as an independent nonprofit organization within the neighborhood. Rev. Royce Hathcock was one of two ministers invited to come from Los Angeles to help get the new idea off the ground. Pulling from much of his L.A. experience, Pastor Royce moved into the neighborhood and began to develop relationships with his neighbors to do the work of community development together. From their earliest days, Neighbor to Neighbor has never begun or ended programs without expressed desire from community members.

Tapestry Church has been one outgrowth of the community's dreams—a result of neighbors expressing a desire for a place of worship where they could fully be themselves. Since 1998, Tapestry has gathered on Sundays at 12:30 for a worship service in which food and play are essential elements of the liturgy. But the congregation and the organization are not easily separated, described as "conjoined twins—joined at the heart." On Sunday the community gathers to worship, and Monday through Saturday they live out their worship together.

In more than twenty years of service, Neighbor to Neighbor has evolved from offering programs aimed to help residents cope with systemic issues to programs that tackle the issues themselves. After decades of offering workforce development and GED classes, they realized there were not enough living-wage jobs to receive the community members who were becoming employable. So they began two businesses that offer a starting income of fifteen dollars per hour.

Rev. Spencer Hathcock, Pastor Royce's son, has witnessed community transformation firsthand since he was a young child. But he only realized how unique and formative his community was after spending four years away at university. "It reignited a desire in me to see the ministry that formed me continue to form others."

Pastor Spencer is adamant that the impact is not one-sided. "It's the community that changes the mentors and volunteers," he says. He has witnessed the truth of the words from Australian Aboriginal artist and activist Lilla Watson: "If you have come here to help me, you are wasting your time, but if you have come because your liberation is bound up with mine, then let us work together."

For Reflection or Discussion

1. What does the mission field of your city need? Is there a particular need you or your team are passionate about and/or have expertise in?
2. Notice which competencies needed for urban church planting listed on page 115 are present in you and/or your team members. How might you gain the competencies you lack, or include others who have them?
3. What churches are doing good work in your city, and how can you partner with them? What challenges and benefits do you see of ecumenical partnerships?

City Practice
Dream with God

We often emphasize the need for plans but neglect the important work of dreaming. Take some time to ask God to share God's dreams for your city as you spend time with these words from the prophet Joel: "I will pour out my Spirit on all people. Your sons and daughters will prophesy, your old men will dream dreams, your young men will see visions. Even on my servants, both men and women, I will pour out my Spirit in those days" (2:28–29). Ask the Spirit to help you imagine what it might look like for this dream to come true in your area. Think of the women and men you know—old, young, privileged and less privileged. What dreams and visions is God giving them? Pray that the dreams of God would take hold and that God would assemble the team needed to bring God's dream into reality.

8

CURRENT MANIFESTATIONS

The Bible offers no specific directions for church planting. The apostle Paul planted churches, but beyond where, when, and why, we know very little about how. Jesus spoke more about the kingdom of God than he ever said about the church. Leonard Hjalmarson surmises that the language of church planting, and the various aspects associated with it, was part of Constantine's legacy and that, viewed through the lens of Christendom, "the boundaries between church and kingdom were blurred." Hjalmarson further maintains that the limitations imposed by the residue of Enlightenment thinking are "fading away in favor of the *missio Dei*."[1] This is not something to fear, for while methodologies and manifestations of the church are cultural—bound by time and place and ever changing—the mission of God is eternal and timeless. There is great comfort in this truth.

Current Manifestations of City Ministries

The Church of the Nazarene in the United States currently has three basic manifestations of city churches located in urban cores: established, immigrant, and compassionate ministries-based. Each of these church types has strengths and weaknesses, and they function best when they work interdependently with

---

1 Leonard Hjalmarson, "Post-Christendom and Adaptive Challenge," in *Text & Context: Church Planting in Canada in Post-Christendom*, ed. Leonard Hjalmarson (Portland: Urban Loft Publishers, 2013), 19.

each other. These three manifestations will be explored, and a possible fourth expression—the parish church model—will also be considered as a viable alternative for planting, developing, and renewing Wesleyan-Holiness churches in the urban context.

ESTABLISHED CHURCHES

Established churches have facilities and membership, both of which are either declining or being renewed. Tim Keller—founding pastor of Redeemer Presbyterian Church in Manhattan and of City to City, a training and networking organization designed to create gospel movements in cities through church planting—believes that one way to renew existing churches is by planting new ones. He suggests four reasons why planting many new churches brings renewal to established churches.

First, "new churches bring new ideas to the whole body of Christ." Because they have the intrinsic freedom to be innovative, new churches become the potential research and development department for every church in the city. Second, "new churches raise up new, creative Christian leaders for the whole city." While older, established congregations may promote stability and tradition, new congregations value creativity and risk, thereby attracting those who have aptitudes and gifts for innovation. These new churches become appealing to the creative artisan class, who have come to the city for the same reasons. Third, "new churches challenge other churches to self-examination."[2] Often it is only in the fruitfulness of new expressions that an established church is forced to consider what is no longer working and the potential value of new wineskins. As demonstrated by Phyllis Tickle and others, this self-examination does not diminish the mother church but strengthens it to imagine a new and better future.[3]

Finally, Keller says that "new churches can be an evangelistic feeder system for a whole community." New life propagates new life. Witnessing life transformation at any level strengthens the whole church. The byproduct is that new

---

2 Timothy Keller, *Center Church: Doing Balanced, Gospel-Centered Ministry in Your City* (Grand Rapids: Zondervan, 2012), 360–61.

3 Phyllis Tickle, *The Great Emergence: How Christianity Is Changing and Why* (Grand Rapids: Baker Publishing Group, 2008), 17. Referring to the inevitable cultural changes that are occurring in the church, Tickle roots cultural upheaval in historical aspects of Christianity that have demonstrated how new expressions of faith do not destroy the existing church but, instead, make it stronger and better. "The organized expression of Christianity which up until then had been the dominant one is reconstituted into a more pure and less ossified expression of its former self."

churches in a city generally bring new people to existing churches. In summary, "vigorous church planting is one of the best ways to renew the existing churches of a city, as well as the single best way to grow the whole body of Christ in a city."[4]

Established churches that have not moved out of the urban core have property and facilities in prime locations. In many instances, precipitously rising costs have made these gentrified areas unaffordable real estate for new congregations. Sharing these facilities with newly birthed congregations can become a means of grace to both the mother church and the newborn church without threatening the viability of either.

Established churches also have material and human resources that church plants may not possess. Christian stewardship demands sharing what has been given by grace with a view for the kingdom of God and without fear of loss—temporally or eternally. A hoarding mindset, for fear that there will never be enough to go around, is both erroneous and anti-kingdom. Established churches that choose generosity have found that there *is* enough, and by giving of themselves, they have discovered renewed life in their own congregations. Moreover, members of established churches are sometimes underutilized and unchallenged in their current congregational settings, and many would relish the opportunity to use their untapped passions and gifts for kingdom service.

IMMIGRANT CHURCHES

Immigrants are some of the most responsive groups in the United States to church-planting and evangelistic efforts. Many arrive with deep religious commitments while others have no church affiliation and are open to the gospel message. Immigrants are often the most overlooked people group in urban settings, yet they may offer the greatest potential for church growth in the United States.

The term "diaspora" refers to displaced people who have migrated, whether freely or by force, from their homeland to another place. Migrants often arrive first in large cities. They come with physical, emotional, and spiritual needs, and they often experience feelings of vulnerability, disorientation, and culture shock. "Their lives have been turned upside-down. They need lots of help, especially in

---

4 Keller, *Center Church*, 361.

the first months and years. If Christians step up to assist them, their hearts can be wide open for the gospel."[5] Helping someone with a great personal need can be perceived as exploitation, or as loving one's neighbor as oneself.

Timothy Smith refers to the act of migration as a "theologizing experience" because those who experience transcultural dislocation from their homeland and former way of life often become aware of God's prevenient and providential grace in a new way. "Their sense of God's care for them intensified as individuals tore themselves loose from rural villages that had once nurtured them."[6] Now they find themselves attempting to acclimate among overwhelming masses in the strange, unfamiliar cultures of new cities. Their survival depends on finding work, a place to live, a school for their children, and a community that will embrace them.

Oliver Phillips, former director of Nazarene Compassionate Ministries and Mission Strategy for the United States and Canada, believes the recent immigration patterns to the United States are the product of divine providence and that they are opening doors for mission opportunities that are unparalleled in history.[7] Phillips is not alone in that opinion. Tom Nees writes in *The Changing Face of the Church*, "As a result of immigration and inevitable global population changes, the cities of the United States and Canada have become as foreign as any so-called foreign country to English-speaking white people who make up ninety percent of the members of the Church of the Nazarene in their countries. It is no exaggeration to describe these urban areas as 'mission fields.'"[8]

As of 2014, almost 40 percent of San Francisco's population was foreign-born. Los Angeles has the multicultural distinction of having no majority population and two hundred different languages spoken.[9] As of 2018, the city of Houston re-

5 Ed Stetzer, "Serving God in Today's Cities: An Interview with Dean Merrill," *Christianity Today*, March 24, 2015, https://www.christianitytoday.com/edstetzer/2015/march/serving-god-in-todays-cities.html.

6 Timothy L. Smith, "Internationalization and Ethnicity: Nazarene Problems and Accomplishments," paper presented to Association of Nazarene Sociologists and Researchers, 1987, ANSR Collection, Nazarene Archives, Global Ministry Center for the Church of the Nazarene, Lenexa, KS.

7 Oliver R. Philips, *Who Moved My Church? New Curves to Express Demographic Changes* (International Church of the Nazarene Multicultural Ministries, 2003), 21, https://www.usacanadaregion.org/sites/usacanadaregion.org/files/WhoMovedMyChurch.pdf.

8 Thomas G. Nees, *The Changing Face of the Church: From American to Global* (Kansas City, MO: Beacon Hill Press of Kansas City, 1997), 84.

9 Cindy Perman, "The Top Ten Most Diverse Cities in America," January 29, 2014, https://www.cnbc.com/2011/05/17/The-Top-10-Most-Diverse-Cities-in-America.html.

ports at least 145 languages spoken, with ninety countries maintaining consular offices.[10] Taking these realities into account, and due to the fact that ministry in the city is now inevitably and indefinitely multicultural, the same missiological strategies and training presented to those who serve as international missionaries would benefit those who serve urban areas in the USA.[11]

Cities presently hold the greatest possibility for fulfilling the Church of the Nazarene's mission, "to make Christlike disciples in the nations." Recognizing rapidly changing demographics, the denomination is attempting to respond to the needs and opportunities presented by migration patterns. "I fear if we [the Church of the Nazarene] continue to do nothing different than we are doing," warns Tom Nees, "in the near future, when and where there is no majority group, this denomination will be marginalized as a predominantly English-speaking white fellowship in a sea of diversity."[12]

In the first multicultural conference of the Church of the Nazarene, General Superintendent Paul Cunningham reflected on witnessing his home church in downtown Chicago leave the city and relocate to the suburbs. The tragedy, for Cunningham, was more than the selling of valuable property that the church would likely never be able to recover; it was leaving the people the church had been birthed to serve. He closed his sermon with a fervent plea to: "Someday we're going to get a vision for the cities. It's missionary work in our cities. We'll not save our cities until we get a missionary vision for the cities. We left the cities, and then the new America moved to the cities. *The mission field decided to come to us, and it came to stay*."[13]

---

10 "About Houston: Facts and Figures," https://www.houstontx.gov/abouthouston/houstonfacts.html.

11 The fact that urban ministry will now certainly be multicultural for an undefined period of time was demonstrated by Nazarene missiologist Paul Orjala in an unpublished paper titled "The Urban Missionary" as part of a Missiologist Committee Report for the Church of the Nazarene, 1996. The concept of an urban missionary was a new way of viewing multicultural ministry in the United States.

12 Tom Nees, "Building an Inclusive Church in a Multicultural Society," unpublished paper, 1999. Quoted in Phillips, *Who Moved My Church?* 22.

13 Paul Cunningham, "There's Room at God's Table for Everyone," sermon, September 1994. Quoted in David M. Best, *The Urban Imperative*, unpublished book commissioned by the Church of the Nazarene Mission Strategy, United States/Canada, 44. Emphasis added.

COMPASSIONATE MINISTRIES-BASED CHURCHES

Compassionate ministries-based churches are the most prevalent Nazarene presence in cities due to the fact that compassion is woven into the ecclesiological fiber of the Wesleyan-Holiness tradition. Similar to eighteenth-century England and nineteenth-century America, cities are home to large numbers of people struggling with economic, physical, and psychological challenges. Hence, for Wesleyans who characterize Christian holiness as best defined as love for God and neighbor, "all our ministry must be 'compassionate ministry.'"[14]

Compassionate ministries-based churches are serious about not only caring for the poor but also addressing the issues and systems that lead to poverty. This type of ministry involves both compassion and advocacy. Compassion is attending to the symptoms of injustice; advocacy is confronting the causes of injustice. Research indicates that, once a driving force of Nazarene church-planting strategies in the city, compassionate ministry centers in the urban core are becoming less tied to local church ministries and more likely to be nonprofit in orientation.[15] What makes compassionate ministries-based churches different from the many other ministries of mercy in the city is the direct connection of compassionate activity with a local congregation. Even their compassionate advocacy is directly linked to the life of a community of faith. Community of Hope in Washington, DC, Los Angeles First Church of the Nazarene, Shepherd Community Center in Indianapolis, and Lower Lights Church of the Nazarene in Columbus are shining examples of this model.

Responding to the Millennial Miracle

The established, immigrant, and compassionate ministries-based Nazarene churches that exist in urban cores are vital and effective, but a new expression is needed for urban church planting in the Wesleyan-Holiness tradition. Currently, a reverse Great Reversal of multiplied thousands are moving back to city centers. Many of them are constituents of the creative class and young adults. An emerg-

---

14   Thomas Noble, "Why the Church of the Nazarene?" sermon (Kansas City, MO: Nazarene Theological Seminary, May 1, 2002).

15   Dale Jones and Rich Houseal, "Urban Cores and the Church of the Nazarene—United States" (Lenexa, KS: Nazarene Research Services for Global Ministry Center for the Church of the Nazarene, July 2015).

ing model of church planting is needed to address the extraordinary millennial migration into urban areas.

In a 2016 exchange with denominational leaders for the Church of the Nazarene, two missional questions were asked: "Where is the church not yet?" and "Who are the unreached people groups in our global regions?" Speaking from the mission context of the United States and Canada, regional director Robert Broadbooks responded that the answers to the questions are intertwined: "The church [in the United States and Canada] is not yet in our great cities, and the unreached people group [in the United States and Canada] are those under the age of thirty-five." In light of the urban history of the Church of the Nazarene, it is clear where the church must return.

Wesleyan-Holiness ecclesiology is mindful of those on the margins, including immigrants, refugees, and the poor. Included in the marginalized of the city are those of varying sexual orientations and gender identity, victims of human trafficking, and those recovering from addiction. Though often not considered a marginalized group, millennials are currently one of the most under-churched, unreached groups in Western society. Their sense of marginalization is often marked with less humility and obvious desperation than other groups, but it exists nonetheless. When Wesleyan-Holiness churches return to the city, they have the potential to address the need for a greater church presence in urban areas as well as the need to reach young adults.

As of 2019, millennials are now the largest generation in American history and, due to immigration, are expected to peak at 76.2 million in 2036.[16] Of course, how one defines the parameters of millennial births will affect how the numbers look and what they mean. Pew Research Center limits the millennial generation to those born between 1981 and 1996. In 1991, Neil Howe and William Strauss—the authors who coined the term "millennials" in their book, *Generations: The History of America's Future*—defined it more broadly than is typically now accepted. Howe and Strauss's millennial generation encompasses those born between 1982 and 2001. Regardless of where the boundary lines are drawn, one thing remains true: millennials are the first generation of the new millennium, and they are being impacted by a rapidly changing world.

---

16   Richard Fry, "Millennials Projected to Overtake Baby Boomers as America's Largest Generation," Pew Research Center, March 1, 2018, https://www.pewresearch.org/fact-tank/2018/03/01/millennials-overtake-baby-boomers/.

American sociologist Robert Wuthnow enumerates seven key trends that are shaping the lives of young adults today:

- delayed marriage
- fewer children and later in life
- uncertainties regarding work and concerns about money
- rising levels of education
- diminished and fewer social relationships
- increased exposure to the forces of globalization
- cultural impact of an information explosion.[17]

As a result of these trends, several sociological behaviors and beliefs among millennials have manifested. First, the racial diversity of the millennial cohort has taught them the value of inclusion and acceptance of a range of cultural and ethnic groups, including a variety of social perspectives. "To this generation, differences are to be praised and honored."[18] This mindset makes millennials skeptical of any way of thinking that dictates conformity in the midst of diversity or that stifles questions about fairness or justice for the oppressed.

Second, millennials are suspicious of organized religion. This fact is more than anecdotal analysis; statistics confirm it. Adults between the ages of 21 and 45 make up at least 40 percent of the adherents of every major faith tradition in the United States. However, younger adults make up a smaller proportion of the adherents of several faith traditions now than they did a generation ago, including a dramatic decrease in the proportion of evangelicals in their twenties. Further, the category of Americans who claim no religious affiliation has the largest proportion of millennials by a significant margin, showing a rise from 1 in 11 to 1 in 5 in the space of a single generation.[19] When asked about the positive impact that churches have in the country, only 55 percent of millennials responded favorably, an 18-percentage-point drop from five years prior.[20]

Third, millennials are seeking a firm moral ground in a relativistic and nihilistic culture. Social scientist Robert Putnam has written about the "judge not"

---

17 Robert Wuthnow, *After the Baby Boomers: How Twenty- and Thirty-Somethings Are Shaping the Future of American Religion* (Princeton, NJ: Princeton University Press, 2007), 20–49.

18 Elisabeth A. Nesbit Sbannato, "Context and Connection: Understanding Generations as Cultures," *Evangelicals Magazine*, Spring/Summer 2017, 16.

19 Wuthnow, *After the Baby Boomers*, 72–77.

20 Hannah Fingerhut, "Millennials' Views of News Media, Religious Organizations Grow More Negative," Pew Research Center, January 4, 2016, https://www.pewresearch.org/fact-tank/2016/01/04/millennials-views-of-news-media-religious-organizations-grow-more-negative/.

mentality that is widespread among young adults and what happens to a society that does not hold others to a moral standard.[21] *New York Times* columnist David Brooks contends that, when it comes to multiple generations of family break-down, "it [is] increasingly clear that sympathy is not enough. It [is] not only money and better policy that are missing in these circles, it [is] norms." These norms, Brooks continues, will require reintroducing "a moral vocabulary," that is, "basic codes and rules woven into everyday life" that offer an alternative to the "*plague of nonjudgmentalism*, which refuse[s] to assert that one way of behaving [is] better than another."[22] The church can provide principled boundaries for a generation desperate for meaning.

Fourth, millennials care deeply about authenticity. They prefer to be real over being relevant.[23] The source or origin of things matters to them. Nina Schmidgall says, "They show their preference for things that are organically grown, locally sourced, sustainable, and traceable." The accoutrements of the church-growth movement, such as "fog machines, large personalities, and performance-driven productions are not attractive" to young adults who yearn for simplicity and honesty. On the contrary, millennials who express interest in the church are "drawn to the anchors of the historic faith." They gravitate toward "ritual, sacraments, and the purity of spiritual disciplines, and are attracted to authentic relationship with God," and they desire to expose their children to the same.[24]

Fifth, millennials are accustomed to rapid and continuous change. With the rise of the internet, millennials are also the first generation to have gained nearly unlimited access to information. They have grown to accept and expect constant motion and continuous change. This reality mandates that the church emphasize a consistent path of discipleship that goes beyond simple conversion, and that any focus on spiritual formation must first be based on authentic relationships. In this respect, Elisabeth Sbanotto advises, "Millennials remind the church that the gospel is about relationship, restoration, unity, and any attempts

---

21　See Robert D. Putnam, *Our Kids: The American Dream in Crisis* (New York: Simon & Schuster, 2015).

22　David Brooks, "The Cost of Relativism," *New York Times*, March 10, 2015, https://www.ny-times.com/2015/03/10/opinion/david-brooks-the-cost-of-relativism.html.

23　Gabe Lyons, *The Next Christians: Seven Ways You Can Live the Gospel and Restore the World* (Colorado Springs: Multnomah Books, 2010), 181–202. Lyons employs the phrase "countercultural, not relevant," to describe millennial attributes.

24　Nina Schmidgall, "Building Faith: Reaching the Next Generation of Families," *Evangelicals Magazine*, Spring/Summer 2017, 18.

at evangelism and discipleship must begin with these things. They challenge hypocrisy and value expressions of faith that are messy, in process, and include the opportunity to express deep doubt."[25]

Sixth, and closely related to the previous point, millennials desire intergenerational connections. Many young adults raised in a church environment were separated from the older generations for programming and worship. They were provided with children's pastors and youth pastors and age-specific events. Only on rare occasions were they given the opportunity to mix with seasoned and saintly older adults, depriving them of the chance to "see faith displayed across generations."[26] The research of Fuller Youth Institute reveals that young people who have shared intergenerational experiences with other people of faith tend to have higher levels of spiritual maturity themselves.[27] Accountability and mentoring are highly valued among millennials.

Thousands of young adults are moving into revived, often gentrified, urban-center neighborhoods. They have been called the "new urban intelligentsia" and remain the "single most unchurched demographic in America today."[28] Their being located where the church is not expresses the critical nature of urban church planting today.

Missional Communities

A shift is taking place between the Christendom-based approach of the attractional church (invitation-based, corporate gathering) and the post-Christendom approach of the incarnational church (culturally based, corporate sending).[29] The established/inherited approach is focused on attractional church methodologies (bring-a-friend Sundays, Christmas pageants, inviting neighbors to attend), while the incarnational approach is focused on existential and incarnational methodologies (coffee shop ministry, smaller gatherings, neighborhood home groups).

---

25 Sbanotto, "Context and Connection," 17.

26 Schmidgall, "Building Faith," 19.

27 See Kara E. Powell and Chap Clark, *Sticky Faith: Everyday Ideas to Build Lasting Faith in Your Kids* (Grand Rapids: Zondervan, 2011). See also Kara Powell, Jake Mulder, and Brad Griffin, *Growing Young: Six Essential Strategies to Help Young People Discover and Love Your Church* (Grand Rapids: Baker Books, 2016).

28 Quote attributed to Ron Benefiel in Best, *The Urban Imperative*, 50.

29 Url Scaramanga and Andy Rowell, "Missional vs. Attractional: Debating the Data," *Christianity Today*, December 2008, https://www.christianitytoday.com/pastors/2008/december-online-only/missional-vs-attractional-debating-data.html.

The problem with this dichotomy is that it projects an either-or mentality while, in reality, all churches should recognize the need for both. The best of the attractional mode's methods combined with the best of the incarnational mode's methods produces missional communities of faith. Missional communities stand at the intersection between attractional and incarnational expressions. Hjalmarson points out that, if missional communities are true to their intended purpose, they *do* gather and *are* attractive.[30]

Missional communities are welcoming and engaging, inviting and sending, converging and dispersing. "Missional communities exist in the same rhythm that exists in the life of the Trinity: inward in love, outward in mission. The overflowing love of life in community results in mission."[31] A renewed expression of church planting is needed to demonstrate the best of missional community in the context of urban neighborhoods. Missional communities will be explored in the next chapter through the parish church model.

A Church for the City
Kirche in Aktion (Wiesbaden, Germany)

The first time Rev. Robert Stoesser was invited to a *Kirche in Aktion* worship service, he admits he went mostly because it was being held in his favorite restaurant in his hometown of Frankfurt, Germany (see chapter 4 for more on the beginnings of KIA in Germany). Stoesser was baptized as an infant and attended Catholic services for several years, but by the time he first attended a *Kirche in Aktion* service he describes himself as having been more of a spiritual person than a Christian. Yet he was excited by the work of this group of Christians, and he quickly became a regular participant in their Community on Mission projects, worship services, and even mission trips outside the country.

Stoesser's pastors called on him to use his expertise in business and marketing, inviting him deeper into the mission and into knowing and following Jesus. Pastor Robert's call to ministry came not long after he decided to fully follow Christ, when a new business enterprise fell apart and he knew he was meant to use his gifts for the church. He began a graduate program in theology and was

---

30 Hjalmarson, "Post-Christendom and Adaptive Challenge," 21.
31 Hjalmarson, "Post-Christendom and Adaptive Challenge," 21.

soon invited to lead a KIA congregation that had begun just two years prior in the nearby city of Wiesbaden.

Not long after moving there, Pastor Robert found there was a surprisingly large number of Iranian and Afghani refugees in and around the city. The church began hosting welcome dinners for refugee families in the cafe where they worshiped, and that was the beginning of long-lasting friendships that grew into a Farsi-speaking congregation less than a year later. When they recognized a need for a Farsi-speaking service, Pastor Robert and his co-pastor, Daniel Atkins, offered to alternate the language each week, with German one week and Farsi the next. But he found that the format of the service changed with the language as well because the Farsi speakers of Muslim background had so many questions that they were eager for discussion during the sermon.

In an often heated, anti-immigrant political climate, the German and Farsi congregation of sixty has certainly witnessed heaven coming to earth in their midst. "Our resettled refugee neighbors put us to shame with the hospitality they extend," says Pastor Robert. And the German congregants have been eager to learn from their Iranian and Afghani neighbors, a handful of whom come to the Farsi service to learn the language. About half of the Farsi-speaking congregants now come to the German service as well, even though they don't know German yet, because they don't want to wait two weeks between services.

Pastor Robert has also learned a new language for communicating the gospel to people who have only ever known Islam. As a student of their honor-shame culture, he is purposeful in creating a space where people can shed their shame. He provides analogies from soccer about learning to play with Jesus as the coach, and he gives people the freedom to use a worship service to "try on" Christianity, like one tries on clothes in a dressing room before buying them. "But in baptism," he says, "you get a full change of clothes."

The city of Wiesbaden has traditionally been a center of healing in the region, getting its name from the natural hot springs that have been drawing people to the town since as far back as the Roman Empire. The KIA Wiesbaden church has incorporated this history into their own story as they partner with God to provide healing to all in their city.

For Reflection or Discussion

1. Consider the different types of urban churches described in the first part of this chapter. What congregations in your city would you consider to be established, compassionate ministry-based, or immigrant community-focused? What does each of these congregations do well, and how might you learn from and/or partner with one or more of them?

2. What is most surprising or challenging to you about the millennial generation, which some would consider the largest unreached people group in the United States?

3. For millennials who care deeply about authenticity and action, being on mission is attractive. How might this shift in thinking produce change in the church?

City Practice
Cross-Cultural Experience[32]

This week, go out of your way to spend time somewhere where the dominant culture is different from your own. Shop at an international market or grocery store. Worship with a congregation where the majority of people don't share your skin color or language. Eat at a restaurant where the menu isn't printed in English. Notice what makes you feel uncomfortable and what makes you feel welcome. Be an observer of the differences, but work hard not to judge whether something is better or worse than what you're used to. Ask the Spirit to help you see God at work in places and languages you don't understand. Pray also that you will have a renewed desire to provide hospitality and compassion to those who feel they don't belong in the places you normally go.

---

32 Based on Michaele LaVigne, *Living the Way of Jesus: Practicing the Christian Calendar One Week at a Time* (Kansas City, MO: The Foundry Publishing, 2019), 189.

9

THE PARISH CHURCH

The new expression of missional communities that is faithful to the Wesleyan-Holiness tradition is the parish church model—churches that are connected to a place and a people by walkable geography and relational networks. The parish is a geographical space in which a church operates. When John Wesley said, "I look upon all the world as my parish," he did not mean that the world was his church; he meant that the whole world is the geographical space in which he would willingly share the transforming grace of God.[1] It is unlikely that Wesley believed he would travel the world and preach the gospel. Rather, this was Wesley's way of saying that the gospel never should be relegated to a particular church or confined to a building. It was a missional statement that affirmed Wesley's idea of the church being a sent people. Henry Knight and Doug Powe agree: "'The world is my parish' is a claim that frees the gospel from the walls of the physical church."[2]

The current evangelical mindset has often extracted Christians from the host culture into the safety zone of the local church. This strategy serves the dual purpose of protecting from the potential dangers of a secular lifestyle and of maintaining the programs and infrastructure of the church. While there are occasional forays back into the culture for evangelistic opportunities and service, the idea is to extract other people from the host culture and bring them into the safety zone

---

1 John Wesley, *Journal* (June 11, 1739), in *The Works of the Rev. John Wesley, A.M.,* ed. Thomas Jackson (London: Wesleyan Methodist Book Room, 1872; reprinted Grand Rapids: Baker Book House, 1979), 19:67.

2 Henry H. Knight III and F. Douglas Powe, Jr., *Transforming Community: The Wesleyan Way to Missional Congregations* (Nashville: Discipleship Resources, 2016), Kindle Location 522.

of the church as quickly as possible. The unintended result of this way of thinking is the disengagement of Christians from the neighborhoods where they live and work and, even worse, a distancing from their non-Christian neighbors.

A parish church model rejects the mindset of extraction and embraces the way of incarnational lifestyles. Just as Jesus became incarnate as "the Word [made] flesh and blood, and moved into the neighborhood" (John 1:14, MSG), so a parish church is about moving into and staying in a neighborhood. Incarnational church planting is more than a sending—it is an indwelling. It is more than a going to—it is a living among.

While reaching an entire city for Christ is a worthy goal, a Wesleyan-Holiness approach considers localities. Instead of thinking more generally of church planting in a metropolis, a Wesleyan-Holiness model will begin to focus on planting churches in neighborhoods. Cities are a complex network of many different neighborhoods, each of which requires careful exegesis and contextualization. What might be effective in one part of a city may be ineffective in another area. A Wesleyan-Holiness approach might plant a neighborhood church in Wicker Park, rather than greater Chicago, or in the Sandton area of Gauteng, rather than greater Johannesburg, or near the high-rise apartments on 5th Avenue and Pine Street. This approach repositions the church as somewhere that one *lives* rather than somewhere one *goes*.

Diana Butler Bass encourages the recovery of the practice of place through a village parish. She describes the historical practice of the parish as a local church serving its immediate community. The pastor and the people of the parish were intimately connected with the life of the village, positioned as a centering point of hospitality and charity.[3] Focusing on geographical community in an intensive way is more decentralized than the common model of established, centralized churches.

The advantages of the parish church concept in the urban context are plentiful. Smaller communities in close proximity can enable their members to connect with each other in a more intimate fellowship of sharing life together throughout the week rather than Sunday alone. The problem of identifying large meeting spaces that provide for parking is also minimized when the group does not require venues that can host a crowd and when members can walk to

---

3 Diana Butler Bass, *Christianity for the Rest of Us: How the Neighborhood Church Is Transforming the Faith* (San Francisco: HarperSanFrancisco, 2006), 38.

gathering points. The parish church model allows each group to "think contextually and uniquely about service, ministry, and evangelism in their respective neighborhoods." When people give, serve, and invest in their local neighborhood context, it can heighten their level of commitment and strengthen the bond between the parishioners and their neighbors. This allows for incarnational ministry "because it maximizes the knowledge about a neighborhood that the people who live there will have."[4]

The parish church model of church planting opts for a geographically based, rather than a demographically based, focus. It will not ignore specific groups that require particular concentration, but its focus will be on the broader heterogeneity of the neighborhood as a whole. While the homogeneity of demographics may enable more rapid numerical growth, it also has a downside: "It has the effect of making the church a subset of secular society rather than a manifestation on earth of the kingdom of Christ."[5]

Because this model is based on the conviction that each local parish has spiritual responsibility for a specific geographical area, then proximity, permanence, and interdependence are crucial to attain neighborhood transformation.[6] Reflecting on the idea of recapturing the parish church model, Leonard Hjalmarson offers an alternative to extraction and an invitation to incarnation: "The parish does not exist in the dualistic, insulated, and protective mode common to Western evangelical churches: it makes the concerns of the [neighborhood] its own concerns. Neither does it exist in the individualistic conversion mode of the typical evangelistic church: its goal is less the conversion of individuals, although this is a good thing, and more the transformation of the [neighborhood]."[7]

Based on the assumption that a local congregation is invested in and cares for the community in which it exists, one urban church network refers to the incarnational presence in local neighborhoods as "retelling the story of Jesus,

---

4 The V3 Church Planting Movement, "3 Ways the Parish Model Would Change Your Church," n.d., https://thev3movement.org/2017/05/18/3-ways-parish-model-change-church/.

5 Edmund P. Clowney, *Living in Christ's Church* (Suwanee, GA: Great Commission Publications, 1986). Quoted in Timothy Keller, *Center Church: Doing Balanced, Gospel-Centered Ministry in Your City* (Grand Rapids: Zondervan, 2012), 369.

6 Awaken Parish Network, "Parish Model Church Planting," n.d., https://static1.squarespace.com/static/590b363bd1758ef7fcc4a2bf/t/59dccdb1f6576e8869fc3094/1507642808182/Parish+Model+Church+Planting.pdf.

7 Leonard Hjalmarson, "Post-Christendom and Adaptive Challenge," in *Text & Context: Church Planting in Canada in Post-Christendom*, ed. Leonard Hjalmarson (Portland: Urban Loft Publishers, 2013), Kindle Location 293.

practicing the way of Jesus, and announcing the way of Jesus."[8] The serving aspect of this parish model is based on two important questions, followed by a purpose statement of: "What if the church saw itself engaged in a loving relationship with its neighborhood? What would it look like for the church to 'romance' the city it worshiped in? To this end, each congregation will seek to discern the ways in which God is active in its community, and then attempt to partner and get involved."[9]

Incarnational, geography-based ministry maintains that place really matters. "It's a way of saying, 'I believe in the incarnation.' Having an earthy eschatology is part of it."[10] Urban pastor Ray Cannata maintains that loving our neighbors begins where they live. "The parish church seeks to be a part of God's answer for the neighborhood. That means that we raise the bar on involvement. We ask members to be very engaged in ministry. We ask, 'Are you willing to make a neighborhood's issues your issues by being salt and light here?'"[11]

The greatest impact of being salt and light in an urban space requires a community of faith working together. The parish church model is a viable way for the body of Christ to move into a neighborhood. It is not only essential to reach urban neighborhoods for Christ, but it is also perfectly aligned with Wesleyan-Holiness ideas of church.

---

8 Awaken Parish Network, "Parish Model Church Planting."

9 Awaken Parish Network, "Parish Model Church Planting."

10 Melissa Kelley, "Redefining the Parish Model: An Old Concept Finds Revival Within the PCA," *By Faith: The Online Magazine of the Presbyterian Church in America*, No. 35 (June 1, 2012), https://by-faithonline.com/redefining-the-parish-model-an-old-concept-finds-revival-within-the-pca/.

11 Cannata is quoted in Kelley, "Redefining the Parish Model."

Parish Church Exemplar:
8th Street Church of the Nazarene

One Nazarene congregation that has adopted the urban parish church model is the 8th Street Church in Oklahoma City, Oklahoma. Eighth Street was launched as a church plant in November 2015, but the dream for it was envisioned several years prior.[12] Recognizing that the midtown/downtown area of Oklahoma City lacked a Wesleyan-Holiness presence, Pastors Chris Pollock and Michaele LaVigne began to dream of planting a church in the heart of Oklahoma City. Both Pollock and LaVigne have shared with me in written and verbal form about how that dream began to take shape and what the fruits of their labor have been.

After many years of neglect, downtown Oklahoma City was being revitalized and began to re-emerge as the epicenter of commerce, economics, entertainment, art, music, and residential life. In 2013, there were approximately forty Nazarene churches in the surrounding Oklahoma City metropolitan area. Yet, in the downtown area with the highest population, there were only five Nazarene congregations. One exceeded eighty in weekly worship attendance; the other four averaged fewer than twenty.[13]

Recognizing the need for a new expression, Pollock began to develop a plan of action for an urban church plant that was presented to the potential mother church. His prospectus highlighted three general reasons why dynamic new churches are necessary: (1) new churches best reach the lost and unchurched; (2) new churches best reach new generations and new people groups; and (3) new urban churches best follow the New Testament pattern and the pattern set in the Church of the Nazarene. Additionally, Pollock proposed four context-specific reasons why this church plant was necessary: (1) the vocational call of the Church

---

12   The 8th Street Church was originally launched under the name of Midtown Church of the Nazarene. The name was changed after the congregation made the move to its current location. The adoption of the name 8th Street Church had three reasons: First, there was a specific commitment to restore a historical building in Oklahoma City because of the related commitment to the parish church model. Additionally, for more than a hundred years, the building has been known as "the church on 8th Street," or "the old 8th Street church." Honoring history is important to the 8th Street Church leaders. Second, the name easily describes the location, which is significant as it pertains to the parish model. Finally, in the story of creation, God created in six days and rested on the seventh. But on the eighth day, God began to create anew.

13   Chris Pollock, "Oklahoma City Church Plant Prospectus: A Proposal to the Bethany First Church of the Nazarene Church Board," October 2013. (Shared personally with author from Pollock, November 2015.)

of the Nazarene is to strategically move toward unreached people groups; (2) it is important to reflect and remain faithful to our heritage; (3) Oklahoma City exerts influence in the wider culture; and (4) there is a spiritual indifference to the gospel, and young adults are a generation in crisis.[14]

The young adult question, for Pollock, revolved around the fact that "younger adults have always been disproportionately found in newer congregations" and that "emerging adulthood is a time of exploration, and generally speaking, during this time in life, commitments are temporary." Pollock went on to say, "Many lack attachments to family members, friends, and personal ideals. It can be assumed, then, without these attachments (indications of a lack of social capital), young adults lack a permanent attachment to a faith community or a set of doctrinal beliefs. . . . Even though Christian spirituality is essentially about relationship and connectedness to God through Christ and others by the work of the Holy Spirit, religion is an isolated and personal subject for most young adults."[15]

Pollock and LaVigne began to imagine a story of hope for the midtown/downtown area through a group of people who did not just attend a church but who would also be committed to *being* the church; who not only gathered as the church on Sunday (attractional) but who also scattered *as* the church throughout the week (incarnational). Pollock wrote,

> Imagine a church where Monday through Saturday is just as important as Sunday. Imagine a people, engaged in community, working together for the glory of God and the good of our city. Imagine little groups of ordinary people scattered all over our city, living missionally in order to bring the light of the gospel in neighborhoods and relational networks—in suburban neighborhoods and big businesses, among artists and mechanics, among medical professionals and international students. Imagine a church that serves as a redeemed community where people find safety, inclusion, healing, and transformation.[16]

The 8th Street parish church model began to take shape around the missiological approach to ministry in which a community of faith is established in a certain area of the city and the Christian story becomes the ethos of the com-

---

14 Pollock, "Oklahoma City Church Plant Prospectus," 4–7.
15 Pollock, "Oklahoma City Church Plant Prospectus," 4–7.
16 Pollock, "Oklahoma City Church Plant Prospectus," 2.

munity. Pollock, who also serves as lead pastor of 8th Street Church, comments, "As God's people we are 'resident aliens' (outsiders) who have been called to care for a location. This concept is holistic, and great effort needs to be made not to be imperialistic."

As a parish-minded church, Pollock maintains that there are three important tasks that the church must engage in. The first task is to "get to know our neighbors." Michaele LaVigne, pastor of spiritual formation for 8th Street Church, agrees: "We have embraced the idea of a parish—of being people of a place, giving care to a specific place with clear geographic boundaries and to the people within them." This approach includes but is not limited to getting to know other established churches and pastors, regardless of denominational affiliation or language group, other non-Christian and Christian faith communities, established business owners, local law enforcement, hospitals and other service-oriented organizations, and nonprofits.

The second task is to "be good neighbors, which begins with listening well." In any existing city, there are already established ministries and community services, but because of a variety of economic, political, and sociological reasons, they do not have enough resources or people to support the work. "A parish model church looks to be good neighbors by discerning the 'good (gospel) work' that others are already doing and getting in on it." According to Pollock, new ministries are not started without considerable listening, discernment, and prayer to allow the parish church to decide on its most appropriate role in the life of the neighborhood.

The third task is to recognize that the "target audience are those who live within walking or bike-riding distance from the place of worship." Pollock explains, "While anyone is welcome, everything that our church does is first and foremost to serve those who live nearby." The incarnational purpose of being good neighbors is why both Pollock and LaVigne chose to move their families to the neighborhood where the church facility is located. LaVigne reiterates this point: "We want to be good and useful neighbors. And we mean 'neighbors' in a very literal sense. We want to know our neighbors—the people who live and work and do life right around us. And we want them to know us as good neighbors who are helpful, who provide care and resources to our neighbors and neighborhood."

The Wesleyan-Holiness parish model adopted by the 8th Street Church is a holistic approach that includes a focus on space, place, and people. In thinking about space, Pollock maintains that the parish model must ask how their property, or worship location, is perceived in the neighborhood. Does it take up resources for self-serving purposes, such as massive parking craters taking over green space? Does the space tell a sacred but good story? Is the space used as a gift to serve the neighborhood by offering sanctuary and safety?

The questions of place are also important to the identity of the parish church model. Pollock asks: Does the location of the church, both building and people, offer resources that indirectly make the place where people live and do life better or worse? Can the people of the missional community imagine their role to be one of redemption? Gentrified neighborhoods bring in money, but are the Christians of that particular context thinking about the services they can establish so that all people in the neighborhood have a chance economically?

If the parish church cares about its parish neighborhood, it will assist people in securing employment. This means starting businesses and training centers as well as offering scholarships and educational opportunities. The questions of people are just as important as the questions of space and place: Does the community of faith advocate for justice among its neighbors? Are they involved in local politics? Do they see themselves in light of the greater Christian story so that equal rights are established in the area? Are the young people given a chance because local schools are supported by the church? Do the people of the congregation speak out against prejudice? The 8th Street Church is still working to advance in this area of ministry.

With this holistic approach to parish ministry, 8th Street Church began meeting in a shared space hosted by another local church in the downtown area until they were able to find a permanent home. LaVigne states that, from the earliest days of the church plant, she and Pollock wanted to focus on several key elements, beginning with seeing an urban building restored. Due to the white flight of the 1970s and '80s, buildings and neighborhoods in midtown with rich histories and intricate architecture were left abandoned and in disarray. "Because we recognize that our God is making all things new," LaVigne explained, "we wanted to participate in this work of making old things new." Pollock underscored this priority: "Early on in this church project, we started to pray for a home for our church. We wanted something with a story that could root us in a neighborhood. Our dream is to reimagine what the church can be—we want to be a people of acceptance and belonging, we want to build a place to gather, pray, tell stories, share struggles, celebrate together, and serve. We call this kind of place a church—which is just another way to say, 'We want to provide a home for those who need it.'"[17]

They found a former Methodist church building on Northwest 8th Street that had been vacant for several years. Constructed by the First German Methodist Congregation in 1907, it is a 7,500-square-foot building built with great care and craftsmanship. A large original oil painting depicting Jesus's walk to Emmaus remains in the church today, along with twenty-two intricate Jacoby stained-glass windows. In 2011, St. Anthony Hospital, located adjacent to the church structure, purchased the building. Conversations began between St. Anthony and the 8th Street Church congregation (then called Midtown Church), and it soon became clear that both were interested in restoring the building and creating a neighborhood church. The hospital offered to sell the building to the congregation for the same price they had purchased it, despite significant gentrification having created rising costs in the immediate neighborhood. In addition, an ongoing partnership of shared services between the church and the hospital was developed for future connections and support.

The young congregation launched a capital campaign to purchase and restore the facility with the tagline, "Let's make something old, new again!"[18] LaVigne points out, "Our desire is to give this building as a gift to the city, and for its restoration to be a physical sign of the restoration we want to see in our parish and our city."[19] Each Sunday for months, congregants shared prayerfully crafted statements surrounding the topic of "My 8th Street Dreams" in a worship service. One member, Evan Mosshart, remarked, "It is a wonderful feeling to restore something to its true glory; to resuscitate and rekindle its vitality. But my dream is more than the building. I dream of a church where we know the people around us—not just their names but the stories of their lives."[20] In 2018, 8th Street Church completed their renovation, restoration, and remodeling project.

---

17 Chris Pollock, "Our 8th Street Dreams," 8th Street Church of the Nazarene, https://www.8thstreetchurch.org/8th-street-project.

18 "8th Street Project," 8th Street Church of the Nazarene, https://www.8thstreetchurch.org/8th-street-project.

19 "8th Street Project."

20 Evan Mosshart, "Our 8th Street Dreams."

A second key element for Pollock and LaVigne was creating connection and community. Connection has to do with real conversations among the members and neighbors that are open, honest, and true to life. LaVigne submits, "We are committed to having real conversations in order to develop real relationships with one another. We want to give people a place to truly belong, and ways to serve. This can only happen when we are intentional about knowing one another, hearing one another's stories, and valuing our differences." In order to do this, 8th Street Church has sought relationships with others who are not like them. LaVigne reiterates, "As a congregation and as individuals, we have developed partnerships and friendships with churches and city leaders who are not like us— those who do not share our same skin color, economic background, language, or even our theology." The church has made it a priority to gather monthly for eating, fun, and shared experiences. The vision statement of 8th Street Church includes, "We will foster real relationships by having real conversations with one another through our worship services, parish groups, and parties."[21] The church is looking for every opportunity to foster true connection and relationship.

Another important facet is what Pollock and LaVigne have called "walking the way of Jesus."[22] LaVigne comments, "Because Jesus provides us with a new way to do life, this is the way we want to walk together. We want to be people of actions, not just words." These actions include holy practices such as worship, parish groups, and service in the Wesleyan-Holiness tradition.

With regard to worship, 8th Street Church has committed to following the Christian seasons, lectionary texts, and ancient creeds to shape their weekend worship services. Pollock believes these commitments have "allowed us to understand the big picture of the story of God we are invited into." The sacraments are regularly celebrated and openly highlighted as means of grace that are an "outward sign of an inward grace," where "God does something for us that we cannot do for ourselves."[23]

Each week the Eucharist is the culmination of the worship service and is an open table, "which means that everyone who is open to the good work of Jesus is invited to receive the bread and wine at Communion," whether they be members of the church or not. Nonalcoholic wine and gluten-free bread, both clearly

---

21 8th Street Church of the Nazarene, "Our Vision," https://www.8thstreetchurch.org/our-vision.
22 8th Street Church of the Nazarene, "Our Vision."
23 "The Eucharist," 8th Street Church of the Nazarene, https://www.8thstreetchurch.org/worship.

advertised, are served so that there are no hindrances for anyone. The worship leader often makes a connection to the denominational history of the Church of the Nazarene by saying, "Historically, our denomination has been rooted in helping people with addictions . . . [like our early founders], we want there to be no barriers."[24] All of the 8th Street Church worship services are intergenerational, and strive to be artistic and purposeful, with special care given to being rooted in Scripture, tradition, reason, and experience.

The practice of telling good stories happens each week during 8th Street Church worship. The gathered community proclaims their identity and mission with a responsive reading marked by its clarity and poetry. A designated, always different, leader—whether a child, a senior adult, or someone in between—will say:

> Hi, my name is [_____], and I'm here because [_____
> _____]. Please hear and respond to
> these words today. We gather here to tell the truth: We don't have
> our lives together. And on our own we can't get them together. We
> confess that we are poor, and we are hungry and thirsty for what
> we cannot provide ourselves. We need God's grace, and we need
> each other. We gather here to tell the truth: that while we were
> still sinners, God died in solidarity with us. And now you and I are
> forgiven, set free, and adopted into a good family. You and I are not
> alone—we belong to God and to one another. We are God's people,
> people who are rich and satisfied, a people of peace, reconciliation,
> and love.
>
> *People: Because Jesus has been the very best neighbor to us, we will be*
> *good neighbors to one another.*
> *All: So today we gather here to tell the truth: our lives are better*
> *when we are neighbors.*
> *People: We will help one another in real ways, and we will have real*
> *conversations with one another.*
> *Leader:* We are not all the same, but we are all ready for transfor-
> mation.
> *People: So let's do the very real and good work of God—together.*
> Leader: We gather here to tell the truth:

---

24 "The Eucharist," 8th Street Church of the Nazarene, https://www.8thstreetchurch.org/worship.

> *All: We will be a spiritual community of hope and transformation that lives the way of Jesus!*[25]

Following this responsive reading, the reader will invite the congregation to participate in the following good-neighbor practice:

> Each week we say these words about who we want to be, but we also take on practices to help us become who we want to be. In just a minute we will have three minutes to talk to one another. So, right now, look around the room. Find a kid or an adult you don't know well, someone you haven't seen in a while, or someone you've never seen before. For ninety seconds, you will tell that person about yourself—who you are, what you love, and why you're here. Then you can hear about them. We'll give you a few seconds to find someone, and then there will be a countdown clock on the screen so you know how long you have.[26]

Following the three minutes of conversation, one of the pastors introduces the week's storyteller. Each week one parishioner shares a five-minute testimony of their life story, including how they came to 8th Street Church and why they have chosen to make it their faith community.

The 8th Street Church walks the way of Jesus by meeting in parish groups throughout the week. These groups meet in neighborhoods throughout the community and are made up of people who live near one another. LaVigne notes: "Parish groups exist to care for one another and to work together to care for others as we learn how to walk the way of Jesus together. This is where we as individuals and as a corporate body figure out together how to really do the things we say we want to do: being good and useful neighbors, connecting and finding community with others, being part of the good work of God that happens all around us." The concept of individuals "figuring out how to really do the things we want to do" is aligned with the Wesleyan practice of the class meeting. The 8th Street Church recognizes that accountability to a parish group is a strong motivation for what happens in a person's life through the week. Holy practices are regular disciplines that spiritually form believers; these practices are

---

25 Weekly worship bulletin for 8th Street Church of the Nazarene, May 2015.
26 Michaele LaVigne, personal email to author, February 6, 2020.

sustained by ongoing accountability to people we are responsible for and who are responsible for us.

The service component of 8th Street Church includes a commitment to serving the people of their immediate parish neighborhood. Many of these neighbors are poor, homeless, and mentally disabled. This commitment to the poor and marginalized is explicitly stressed in 8th Street Church's media and marketing language: "In its earliest days, our denomination started churches in the urban core and was focused on three things: a commitment to cities and the poor, active involvement in social issues, a doctrine of hope. Our desire is to return to these essential issues by being a faithful presence in midtown/downtown."[27] Pollock believes that ministry to and with the poor is a means of grace that is necessary for the spiritual formation of the congregation and of their neighborhood parish. Pollock adds, "We have found that as we engage our neighbors—especially those not like us—we are the ones being transformed, which I think is the essence of Wesley's social ethic."

The 8th Street Church is investigating, considering, and dreaming of the development of a nonprofit for acquiring commercial real estate. The properties would be places where they can improve the area and work with young entrepreneurs to begin service-oriented, for-profit businesses that would both improve the economy of the neighborhood and create jobs within walking distance of the church. Pollock states, "I am coming to believe that for the people in our area, the best way to Jesus is through a job." The locations of the businesses would become potential new start locations for more churches.

Exposure to the poorest of the city becomes a matter of essential discipleship for urban dwellers in the parish church expression of Wesleyan-Holiness ecclesiology, and is connected to 8th Street Church's vision for connecting with their young adult neighbors. Even though 8th Street Church's parish is experiencing some characteristics of gentrification, it continues to maintain aspects of an inner-ring neighborhood. Sean Benesh offers a vision for parish church plants in inner-ring neighborhoods: "I see Christians and churches embodying a more incarnational presence in the neighborhood, seeking its *shalom*, and being more organic in their liturgical expression. They [would be] intentionally identifying

---

27 8th Street Church of the Nazarene, "Our Beliefs," https://www.8thstreetchurch.org/our-beliefs.

with the poor and marginalized. These kinds of churches are needed because they reflect the dynamics of their neighborhoods."[28]

This attitude is the opposite of moving into gentrified, "cool, hip, trendy" neighborhoods, which much of the creative class is wont to do. The parish church model is the incarnational way that more deeply displays the *raison d'être* of the Church of the Nazarene and for the vision of 8th Street Church. As Kenneth Carder affirms, these mutually beneficial relationships of the poor with the community of faith may be the saving grace of the parish church model.[29] It can also be a test for the hermeneutic of love. Benesh says, "It is easy to love a city and parts of the city that are beautiful, well-maintained, and safe. When cities are undesirable, dangerous, and wild our love is truly tested."[30]

The 8th Street Church is a stellar example of the parish church model within the Wesleyan-Holiness tradition. The church is finding a way to take the unique qualities of Wesleyan-Holiness theology and incorporate them into essential practices of Wesleyan-Holiness ecclesiology. While one form of the parish church model does not require duplication, 8th Street Church is an exemplar of faithful and sustainable practices that take missional living and incarnational ministry seriously.

A Church for the City
Many Nations Church (Fort Wayne, IN)

Rev. Javier Mandragon remembers a church in his hometown of Cuernavaca, Mexico, near where he and other gang members would hang out to drink. They could hear singing, and often church members walked past them on the way to and from services—but no one ever invited them inside or even spoke to them. Almost everything has changed about Pastor Javier's life since then, but the memory of that church still remains. Now as a pastor himself, he is determined that no one will have that experience in his church's neighborhood. "We will not only open our doors," he says, "but we will actively pursue them and tell the story that can change their lives now and forever."

---

28 Sean Benesh, *Exegeting the City: What You Need to Know about Church Planting in the City Today* (Portland: Urban Loft Publishers, 2015), Kindle Location 666.

29 Kenneth L. Carder, "What Difference Does Knowing Wesley Make?" in *Rethinking Wesley's Theology for Contemporary Methodism*, ed. Randy L. Maddox (Nashville: Kingswood Books, 1998), 30.

30 Sean Benesh, *Metrospiritual: The Geography of Church Planting* (Eugene, OR: Resource Publications, 2011), 153.

In 2008 the Northeast Indiana District of the Church of the Nazarene invited Rev. Annette and Rev. Javier Mondragon to begin a new church in a high-poverty, predominantly black neighborhood of southeast Fort Wayne. Grace Point Church of the Nazarene, a suburban congregation on the north side of the city, helped launch the church plant. The Mondragons say it has not always been easy raising their children in a neighborhood with high poverty and crime, but they have stayed because they are convinced God wants them to be part of change and healing in that place.

The Mondragons understand that the root of crime is poverty and that the way to fully break the cycle of poverty is to help people find solutions—which is exactly what the church and its partner organization, Bridge of Grace Compassionate Ministries Center, are doing in their neighborhood, Mount Vernon Park. They begin not by asking what is wrong in the community but instead by asking what is good and how it can become better.

Launched in 2011, Bridge of Grace buys and renovates old homes in their low-income area, reselling them at affordable prices to help renters become homeowners. They have also created a neighborhood playground and outdoor gathering space, and they acquire vacant lots for Habitat for Humanity to build new homes. The Many Nations congregation has also led efforts to clean up and increase safety in the neighborhood.

Mount Vernon Park is visibly different than it was when Pastors Javier and Annette arrived in 2008. In 2018 the police department reported the crime rate had dropped by half. Numerous city officials and businesses partner with the work of the church, and in 2019 Pastor Javier was named Citizen of the Year by Fort Wayne's *Journal Gazette*. Yet the Mandragons want to see transformation in all fifty neighborhoods in southeast Fort Wayne: "Our goal is to create a model here that we can replicate in other neighborhoods."

It's easy to see the outward change of the neighborhood, but there's much more than property development going on. The Many Nations congregation provides the heart and soul of the community's transformation, with the local *Journal Gazette* describing it as "the center of a spreading oasis."[31] There are twelve nations represented in the congregation, and all services are held in both English

---

31 Michelle Davies, "Citizen of the Year: Javier Mondragon," *The Journal Gazette*, December 29, 2019, https://journalgazette.net/opinion/20191229/javier-mondragon?fbclid=IwAR3FN4iolwZooc-f6a2sTlpuWKMCGlLDX1xxHrHD-KiurzzUs7gQTrbztqsw.

and Spanish. Together they give witness to a new way of life—a life of unifying love, great hope, and joyful purpose. They not only preach good news, but the pastors and people of Many Nations also *are* good news for the people of Fort Wayne, Indiana.

For Reflection or Discussion

1. When have you witnessed someone following Jesus's example of living *among* a people really well?
2. In your experiences of participating in and/or leading congregations, are you more familiar with a demographically based or geographically based focus? How do these differences play out in day-to-day life and decision making?
3. Considering the example of 8th Street Church, what activities or priorities do you see as unique for a parish-minded congregation?

City Practice
Who Is My Neighbor?

Think about the geographical boundaries of your own parish, beginning with the square mile surrounding your church or home. You may even want to print a map of this area to help you visualize it. Fill in the names of neighbors you already know: individuals, businesses, churches, organizations, schools. Continue to learn who your neighbors are by walking or riding your bike as much as possible through the area and visiting with people you encounter. If there are schools, churches, or other community organizations present, set up a time to meet with these leaders. Use this knowledge to help you pray for and plan well for your parish.

CONCLUSION

The Church of the Nazarene has a history of established, immigrant, and compassionate ministries-based expressions of urban churches. All three of these continue to be needed and will be strengthened by working together. The parish church model has been largely unexplored and untested in Wesleyan-Holiness circles, and will require integration of previous methods with a renewed commitment to a high level of discipleship. A Wesleyan-Holiness ecclesiology is a natural fit for contextual parish church expressions and can be effective in ministering among the creative class and millennials through a strong emphasis on compassion, discipleship, and accountability.

The optimism of grace offers a message of hope and belief in genuine, life-changing conversion and real societal transformation. The eschatological vision of Isaiah 11 is both a picture and paradigm of the kingdom of God in the city. The middle way, or *via media*, position allows for the messiness of the city, both methodologically for mission and structurally for church organization. The peaceable kingdom flexibility that is found in the middle way corresponds to the diversity needed for specific neighborhood contexts.

Finally, a commitment to Christian community is a value for Wesleyan-Holiness ecclesiology that calls for living in proximity to our closest relationships. The power of accountability is needed for growth in holiness. The dangers of individualism, isolation, and too much independence with too little accountability are great. David Fitch underscores the need for community in guiding lifestyle choices: "We now recognize that the consumerist forces of our post-Christendom . . . cannot be resisted as isolated individuals. An individual alone cannot resist the forces of desire that tell us a five-bedroom house and two new cars are more important than mission, the very life we share with the triune God. Our communities, therefore, must be places of spiritual formation, of resistance to the forces of distraction, unsatiated desire, and exploitation of those we choose not to know." The implications for urban church planting in the Wesleyan-Holiness tradition are profound. "Congregations may be especially attractive as places to experience 'community,' when community is harder to find."[1]

Urban discipleship in the Wesleyan-Holiness tradition depends on relationships of integrity, proximity, and intensity. This is a hopeful way forward for urban church planting, development, and renewal in the Wesleyan-Holiness tradition.

---

[1] David Fitch, "50 Years of Church Planting: The Story as I See It," in *Text & Context: Church Planting in Canada in Post-Christendom*, ed. Leonard Hjalmarson (Portland: Urban Loft Publishers, 2013), Kindle Location 649.

THE SYMBOLIC NATURE OF BIBLICAL CITIES

Jerusalem became the biblical archetype of God's hope for a city and the possibilities of urban redemption. It was called "the joy of the whole earth" (Psalm 48:2). It radiated divine presence and power: "From Zion, perfect in beauty, God shines forth" (Psalm 50:2). Jerusalem was even declared to be the desired dwelling place of God: "This is my resting place for ever and ever; here I will sit enthroned, for I have desired it. I will bless her with abundant provisions; her poor I will satisfy with food. I will clothe her priests with salvation, and her faithful people will ever sing for joy" (Psalm 132:14–16). This history importantly details that the city of Jerusalem functioned with a centripetal (directed toward the center) flow of mission. Like a missional magnet, the centripetal force of Jerusalem and her temple drew people to its center for the glory and worship of God. The nations were invited to come to Jerusalem and discover the beauty of monotheism and the corporate life of a holy nation created to glorify and worship the one true God.

Nineveh was another symbolically important biblical city that changed the trajectory of urban mission. As the capital city of the Assyrian Empire, Nineveh was considered the largest city in the world. The book of Jonah describes it as an expansive city that took a full three days to walk across (3:3), and with a population of more than 120,000 people (4:11). But Nineveh was also known for its exceedingly pagan practices. It was a wicked city that deserved God's righteous judgment. It was filled with spiritually blind people "who cannot tell their right hand from their left" (v. 11). They were not seeking God, and they did not care about Jerusalem. So out of merciful compassion, God sent Jonah to them, to go to where they were and preach to them.

Here is a major shift in urban missions that foreshadows the words of Jesus in the Great Commission. The people of God are sent out to be missionaries to the cities of the world. Whereas the previous flow of urban mission had been centripetal, it now became what Timothy Keller has referred to as the centrifugal flow of mission.[1] It became an outward focus with an emphasis on going. It became a movement directed outward from the center. For those unwilling or unable to come and survey the glory of God in Jerusalem, the good news would now be brought to their local neighborhood.[2] The flow of mission had reversed course.

This centrifugal emphasis became even more pronounced when the people of God were taken into Babylonian exile. What was the missional message to God's exiled people in a dangerous and oppressive environment? "Build houses and settle down; plant gardens and eat what they produce. Marry and have sons and daughters; find wives for your sons and give your daughters in marriage, so that they too may have sons and daughters. Increase in number there; do not decrease" (Jeremiah 29:5–6). The exiles were to maintain their identity in a strange land, raise their families, and strive to flourish. They were to increase, not decrease. But they were to do more than increase their own well-being. "Also, seek the peace and prosperity of the city to which I have carried you into exile. Pray to the LORD for it, because if it prospers, you too will prosper" (v. 7).

These words from the prophet Jeremiah were a profoundly significant invitation. The exiles were being asked to do more than seek personal prosperity; they were called to pursue the welfare of the city in which they found themselves. They were to bring the ethic and ethos of Zion to a very great—but very pagan—place. They were to be, as a way of speaking, "resident aliens."[3] They were a missional people who knew they were not yet home but who were called to be committed to living as if they were.

---

1 Timothy Keller, *Center Church: Doing Balanced, Gospel-Centered Ministry in Your City* (Grand Rapids: Zondervan, 2012), 147.

2 Tim Keller, "What Is God's Global Urban Mission?" Lausanne Movement, 2010. I am indebted to Tim Keller for his insights on the centripetal and centrifugal aspects of mission.

3 "Resident aliens" is a term coined by Stanley Hauerwas and William H. Willimon in their book of the same title, *Resident Aliens: Life in the Christian Colony: A Provocative Christian Assessment of Culture and Ministry for People Who Know That Something Is Wrong* (Nashville: Abingdon Press, 1989).

This centrifugal urban movement continued in the early church. All the great cities of the known world became missional targets of vast importance. The political center of the first-century Greco-Roman world was Rome. The commercial center was Corinth. The intellectual center was Athens. The case could even be made that the religious center—with its many temples to pagan gods and imperial worship—was Ephesus. These cities and others like them (Thessalonica, Damascus, Iconium, Philippi, Lystra, Antioch, Caesarea, Galatia, Pergamum, and more) became missional targets for the centrifugal flow of the urban Christian movement.

The missionary journeys of the apostle Paul are well documented. These cities became his singular focus for frontline missionary activity. It was not because Paul had disregard for rural areas. He simply recognized that, if the gospel were able to penetrate society's great cultural centers, it would ultimately spread to the farthest reaches of the empire. Paul spent more than two years in the highly influential city of Ephesus. The kingdom impact was significant. According to Luke's record in Acts, "All the Jews and Greeks who lived in the province of Asia heard the word of the Lord" (19:10). The Christian work in Ephesus flowed with centrifugal force into the surrounding areas. The rest of the New Testament documents read very much the same.

Cities have a prominent place in the history of Christian mission, and hold imminent promise for the importance of the great cities of the world today. This is far more than a vision for urban ministry in North America. The masses of people gathered in cities await the gospel on every continent. There is no one-size-fits-all formula for planting urban churches in diverse cultural contexts, but the tools of Wesleyan-Holiness theology and ecclesiology are adaptable and transferable. As long as the methods do not compromise the message and the mission, we must give permission for flexibility. That "the advent of the New Jerusalem described in Revelation is an urban, rather than pastoral, paradise" continues to speak volumes about the present and coming kingdom of God.[4] And so we pray, *your kingdom come, your will be done, on earth as it is in heaven.*

David A. Busic

Advent 2019

---

4 Abram Lueders, "Evangelicals and the New Urbanism," *Marginalia: Los Angeles Review of Books*, April 22, 2017, https://marginalia.lareviewofbooks.org/evangelicals-new-urbanism/.